Animal Mycophiles

Critters that Hunt, Farm,
Self-Medicate,
& Get High on Fungi

Animal Mycophiles

GREEN WRITERS PRESS *Brattleboro, Vermont*

Critters that Hunt, Farm, Self-Medicate, & Get High on Fungi

EVA GORDON

Printed in the United States

10 9 8 7 6 5 4 3 2

Green Writers Press is a Vermont-based publisher whose mission is to
spread a message of hope and renewal through the words and images we
publish. Throughout we will adhere to our commitment to preserving and
protecting the natural resources of the earth. To that end, a percentage
of our proceeds will be donated to environmental activist groups and
social justice organizations. Green Writers Press gratefully acknowledges
support from individual donors, friends, and readers to help support the
environment and our publishing initiative.

GReen
WRITERS
press

Giving Voice to Writers & Artists Who Will Make the World a Better Place
Green Writers Press | Brattleboro, Vermont
www.greenwriterspress.com

ISBN: 979-8-9923988-4-7

COVER DESIGN BY ALLISON PINEAULT
ILLUSTRATIONS: ISTOCK

PRINTED ON PAPER WITH PULP THAT COMES FROM FSC-CERTIFIED FORESTS, MANAGED FORESTS THAT
GUARANTEE RESPONSIBLE ENVIRONMENTAL, SOCIAL, AND ECONOMIC PRACTICES. ALL WOOD
PRODUCT COMPONENTS USED IN BLACK & WHITE, STANDARD COLOR, OR SELECT COLOR
PAPERBACK BOOKS, UTILIZING EITHER CREAM OR WHITE BOOKBLOCK PAPER
ARE SUSTAINABLE FORESTRY INITIATIVE® (SFI®) CERTIFIED SOURCING.

Contents

Prologue

As I dive onto the forest floor, a surge of excitement reverberates through my veins, while the leaves beneath my fingers disclose their whispered secrets. Today's mushroom foray is a treasure hunt, a thrill akin to spotting a lion on an African safari. Unlike the obvious grace of a zebra on the savanna, mushrooms play a game of hide-and-seek. They erupt from the earth like ephemeral sculptures, often with vibrant splashes of color against the browns and greens. Fungi demand close inspection, a keen eye, and sometimes, a bit of detective work. This isn't just a nature walk; it's a puzzle waiting to be solved. You become a Sherlock Holmes of sorts, putting together all the pieces before declaring the name down to species. But the real magic goes beyond identification. As I weave through the trees, a symphony of birds and insects erupts, a Vivaldi concerto played by the forest itself. Each chirp and buzz soothes my soul, washing away the stresses of daily life. This is nature therapy at its finest, a balm for the weary city dweller.

My passion for the unseen world began in childhood, with tadpoles in creeks and ladybugs in orchards. Bird watching later opened my eyes, not to the skies but to the hidden fungi kingdom on the forest floor. These cryptic mushrooms, like tiny torches, ignited a spark within me. The fascination with fungi took root in my mind, a mycelium of obsession spreading through my thoughts. My home became a library of mushroom guides; my weekends were spent foraging with fellow mycophiles. Soon, I was sharing this passion as an educator, translating the language of fungi for eager minds. Fungi weren't just names on a list; they were architects of the forest, their intricate partnerships with plants sculpting the very landscape.

Little did I know that when I became obsessed with fungi around 2019, mushrooms had already entered the zeitgeist of our times. People were embracing "mycophilia," the love of fungi. Some sought edible delights, while others cultivated their own earthy bounty. But the possibilities went far beyond the dinner plate. Fungi were being hailed as bioremediators, sustainable materials, even fashion statements. And at the heart of it all was the wonder of the mycorrhizal network—a silent web connecting plants and fungi.

Bending low, I watch a slug feast on a fallen mushroom, its slimy body a tiny gourmet relishing its delicacy. Flies swarm another, drawn by the carrion-like stench stench of a "stinkhorn." These phallic fungi, nature's perfumers, use their pungent odor to lure their fly-borne pollinators. Then I see them—tiny worms wriggling between the gills. Curiosity gnaws at me, urging me to delve deeper. Beyond the known world of spore dispersal and insect farms, I sense a vast, unexplored territory—the realm of animal mycophiles. These critters, with their intimate relationships with fungi, are a story waiting to be told.

So, fueled by a love of nature, a thirst for knowledge, and the joy of writing, I embark on this journey to explore the fascinating world of fauna-funga relationships. From the curious habits of insect cultivators to the surprising fungal delicacies enjoyed by forest creatures, I hope to weave a narrative that both informs and inspires.

Animal Mycophiles

Critters that Hunt, Farm,
Self-Medicate,
& Get High on Fungi

Introduction

A Kingdom of Their Own

If you do not know the names of things,
the knowledge of them is lost, too.
~Linnaeus

Fungi aren't just a dusty footnote on our planet's legacy; they're the hidden marvels of our planet's past and future. These silent trailblazers paved the way for life on land back in Earth's early days, and now, after years of being overshadowed by the flashier plant kingdom, they're finally getting their due credit. In 1969, the same year we landed on the moon, scientists finally acknowledged fungi as a separate kingdom, igniting a renewed interest in these often-overlooked wonders. While they might share some plants' vegetative traits, such as the root-like mycelium and the fleeting beauty of mushrooms, fungi are an entirely different organism. Fungi lack the chemistry that plants have to turn sunlight into sugars through photosynthesis. Plants and fungi store food differently; plants store it as starch, while fungi store food as glycogen, similar to animals. They don't bask in the sun as do plants, nor

3

do they boast vibrant blooms or towering forests. Instead, fungi lurk beneath the earth's surface or cling to trees, their unseen work shaping the world.

Animals with their flashy fur, feathers, and fins draw our attention more. We see, hear, and interact with animals every day, from cuddly pets to ants on your pathway. Animals gallop across fields, soar through skies, and dive into oceans, their vibrant forms impossible to miss. But what about the humble fungi, tucked away underfoot or clinging to trees? Despite their muted nature, fungi share a surprising closeness to animals, both in their hidden diet and their evolutionary history. Both are heterotrophs utilizing organic matter for sustenance. While animals rely on internal digestion, fungi take a different approach. Fungi secrete enzymes to dissolve their environment and absorb the nutrients. Don't let the similarities fool you, though.

These two kingdoms exhibit clear dissimilarities. Unlike animals, fungi have a cell wall made of chitin similar to the exoskeleton of arthropods, while animals do not have a cell wall. Another unique feature of fungi is a sterol called ergosterol, which keeps their cell walls strong, while animals have cholesterol, a major component of cell membranes. Animals, with their fancy senses and nervous systems, navigate and react to the world in an instant. Fungi are more laid-back. They lack those fancy organs and brains, and instead, spread their network of hyphae filaments (called mycelium) like a silent explorer, searching for food and space to grow.

Despite America's deep-seated fear of mushrooms, they don't seem to fear the estimated 700 poisonous plant species lurking in the shadows. Mycophobia is giving way to mycophilia, fueled by a growing understanding of the vital roles fungi play in our planet's health. We've been neglectful of these hidden marvels, with less than 5% of all fungal species even identified. But thanks to DNA technology and platforms like iNaturalist and FunDiS, we're finally cracking the code of their classification. Mushroom forays are no longer just for the fearless, but a trendy way to learn, eat, and even grow your own culinary treasures. Their long history as medicine has sparked renewed interest in their potential, while sustainable materials and solutions to pollution problems like heavy metals and plastics are looking to fungi for inspiration. So, ditch the fear and embrace the wonder—the future is looking positively fungal! Imagine a world without lush greenery, vibrant forests, and the very air we breathe. It might seem impossible, but without the silent partners lurking beneath the surface—fungi—this grim reality could be closer than we think. Forget the poisonous stereotypes and creepy myths.

The vast majority of fungi are not our enemies, but vital allies. Their intricate relationships with plants through mycorrhizal fungi are the foundation of our planet's health. Think of it as an underground handshake. Mycorrhizal fungi, like tiny threads, weave themselves around plant roots, forming a vast network known as the mycelial web. This web acts like an extension of the plant's own root system, helping it absorb critical nutrients like nitrogen and phosphorus from the soil. In return, the plant supplies the fungi with energy-rich sugars, a win-win partnership for both. This symbiotic relationship is pervasive. Studies estimate that over 90% of all land plants rely on fungi for survival. While the mycorrhizal relationship is between plants and fungi, it's like a boost for the whole neighborhood. The plants get stronger, and that strength turns into a delicious advantage for animals, especially pollinators. From towering redwoods to delicate wildflowers, these unseen connections are the lifeline of our forests, fields, and even the oxygen we breathe.

But fungi's magic goes beyond just plants. They are the tireless decomposers, the silent sanitation workers of the natural world. From fallen leaves to animal carcasses, fungi break down organic matter, returning vital nutrients to the soil and preventing the buildup of waste. Picture a world without the sweet scent of fallen leaves after rain, or the fertile soil teeming with life. Without fungi's tireless work, our ecosystems would crumble, devoid of the essential nutrients that sustain all forms of life.

The understanding of this hidden web is blossoming. The importance of fungi in forest health has been revealed by books like Susan Simard's *The Mother Tree*. Sustainable forest practices are incorporating mycorrhizal relationships into their strategies, recognizing the importance of nurturing this underground network. This newfound appreciation extends beyond the forest floor. The study of mycology is gaining traction, with applications in agriculture, medicine, and even bioremediation. Fungi's ability to break down pollutants and their potential for producing sustainable materials are just a glimpse of the possibilities they hold. So, the next time you step outside, take a moment to appreciate the unseen heroes beneath your feet. Fungi are not just fascinating organisms, they are the architects of our planet's health, the silent partners of the intricate web of life. Remember, the hidden world of fungi is waiting to be discovered. With each new study and each new appreciation, we unravel the mysteries of this interconnected web, revealing the true heroes of our planet. Let's step into this hidden kingdom, one mushroom at a time, and celebrate the beauty and importance of the fungal world.

While we may often focus on the vibrant spectacle of animals and the towering majesty of plants, a hidden kingdom lies beneath our feet, pulsating with life and shaping the very foundation of our planet's health. This is the Kingdom Fungi, and its relationship with the animal world is a testament to the interdependence that plays out across every ecosystem. Over millennia, fungi and animals have co-evolved, developing a relationship of nutrient exchange and spore dispersal. Tiny beetles cultivate miniature gardens on their backs, feasting on the fungi while spreading their spores across the land. Slugs, with their discerning palates, become living delivery trucks for specific fungi, ensuring their continued propagation. This most fascinating method involves a cast of furry, feathered, and sometimes slimy characters—enter **zoochory**, the art of using animals as spore-spreading taxis. Within zoochory there are two travel options: **endozoochory**, the "scenic route" through digestive systems, where spores are pooped throughout distant lands, and **ectozoochory**, the "sticky-note" version, where spores cling to fur, feathers, or skin. These animal carriers, whether internal or external, are the vectors, the unsung heroes of spore dispersal, ensuring fungal spores get to explore new territories.

Understanding these intricate connections is crucial for preserving the delicate balance of our ecosystems. Animal-fungi relationships play a vital role in nutrient cycling, decomposition, and soil formation. Bees buzz, transferring spores and pollinating. Dung beetles recycle, creating fertile ground for fungal growth. Consider the disastrous repercussions of eliminating just one species from this web. By recognizing these interdependencies, we can prioritize conservation efforts that protect habitats and maintain biodiversity.

Studying these relationships unlocks knowledge for sustainable practices. We can harness beneficial fungi for biological pest control, reducing chemical reliance. Insights of animal-fungi relationships guide pollinator conservation and ecosystem restoration, enhancing resilience. The significant role fungi play in carbon sequestration offers substantial benefits to climate change mitigation strategies. Learning about these relationships provides essential insights into ecosystem functioning and conservation.

Knowing the importance of fungi, can you imagine a world where mushrooms cannot spread their spores? That's the reality for many fungi without a little help from their animal friends! For millions of years, these hidden masters of survival have developed a bag of tricks to hitch a ride and colonize new lands. Some blast their spores into the air like tiny rockets, while others catch a wave on a raindrop.

Forget windblown spores and passive water dispersal. In spreading their spores, fungi are the chefs of the natural world, drawing in animal customers with a tantalizing menu and irresistible ambiance. Envision a mushroom as an upscale restaurant, with vibrant colors and intoxicating aromas like a Michelin-starred menu. But along with gourmet dishes, this restaurant offers a unique cuisine of tiny spores, ready to be carried far and wide by its furry and feathery patrons.

Once a mushroom has 'sprouted', it has a physical location in the same way a restaurant has an establishment where it serves and presents its culinary offerings. Location, location, location. Some mushrooms take advantage of the concept of fast-food restaurants by growing together and appearing everywhere.

Just like any successful restaurant, fungi rely on clever adaptations to attract their animal partners. Forget about boring storefronts—these mushrooms dress to impress, sporting bright reds, oranges, and yellows that scream, "Look at me!" Some even take it a step further, glowing like neon signs with their bioluminescent magic, drawing insects to feast. Michael Pollan, author of *Botany of Desire*, confirms that colors, along with a fleshy nutritious fruiting body, make the fungi more visible to animals. Pollan explains some mushrooms produce toxins that can deter predators and attract the better spore dispersing animals. These toxins are attractive to slugs and snails, critters that will disperse the spores over wide distances. The importance of spore dispersing animals is just coming into play.

And who can resist a delicious aroma? Merlin Sheldrake, author of *Entangled Lives: How Fungi Make Our Worlds, Change our Minds and Shape Our Futures*, explains that some mushrooms have evolved aroma attractants that are tailored to certain animals such as compounds that mimic the scent of pheromones. Mushrooms release a cocktail of volatile chemicals, tempting scents that mimic everything from sweet fruit to decaying flesh, depending on the animal they want to attract. Think pheromone-infused pizza for pigs—these fungi know how to speak their customers' language.

But it's not just about the smell. Some mushrooms offer a sticky, slime-coated texture that clings to feathers and fur, ensuring a free ride to new locations. Others play it safe, popping up in high-traffic areas like the forest floor, where hungry slugs and snails can't resist their tempting treats. And of course, location is everything. Living in a place where mushroom-eating creatures live benefits fungal reproduction. Some fungi even team up, forming clusters like bustling food courts, making it impossible for passing animals to miss their delicious offerings.

The benefits of this partnership are mutual. Animals get a nutritious snack, while fungi get their spores dispersed across vast distances, colonizing new habitats and ensuring their survival. This unique dining experience redefines fast food by offering a trendy open-air restaurant where mushrooms play the role of chefs and customers become unsuspecting heroes of the fungi kingdom.

Fungi are top marketers, culinary geniuses, and testaments to the incredible partnership that shapes our world. Remember, these hidden restaurants are more than just fungi—they're the architects of our ecosystems, reminding us that even in the hidden corners of nature, a delicious drama unfolds. It's no wonder why so many animals from industrious insects to furry mammals and even feathered friends, have developed a taste for fungi. This love affair, known as *mycophagy* (from Greek *mykes*, meaning mushroom and *-phagy* meaning eating from the Greek *phagein*) isn't just a culinary delight; it plays a crucial role in keeping the forest floor balanced by regulating fungal populations.

This love of edible mushrooms has led some animals to practice mushroom farming known as **fungiculture**, or **mycoculture**. Forget foraging for wild mushrooms—social insects like leaf-cutting ants are expert **farmers**, cultivating their own personal mushroom farms! These industrious creatures meticulously cut and transport leaves, creating the perfect environment for their fungal partners to thrive. The ants get a nutritious snack and the fungi get a safe place to grow and spread their spores. It's a win for everyone.

While studies have shed light on the amazing partnerships between animals and fungi, like spore-spreading zoochory, mycophagy, and mushroom farming (myco-cultivation), this field is still young and hungry for more research. We need to understand these animal mycophiles (fungi fans) and their favorite fungi better!

Appreciating these intricate relationships helps us see nature's delicate balance. And guess what? We humans are animals too, playing a role in mycophagy, zoochory, and mycocultivation. Throughout history, *Homo sapiens* have savored edible mushrooms, a valuable source of food for hunter-gatherers, especially when the weather wasn't playing nice. When we forage for these tasty treats, we're helping spread their spores, just like tossing away apple seeds after a delicious snack. This human-powered spore dispersal is called anthropochory. And get this—DNA evidence from Neanderthal tartar shows they were big mushroom fans too, proving our fascination with fungi goes way back!

Before I delve into how animals find hidden fungi, let's take a fascinating detour to explore how critters perceive the world. Forget rigid landscapes and objective realities—animals experience their environment through a unique lens, a subjective realm shaped by their senses and mental processes. This personalized "umwelt," as biologist Jakob von Uexküll called it, is a world where, for example, a dog's nose paints a vibrant portrait of hidden scents, and a bee sees not just flowers, but glowing guides to sweet nectar. Understanding this *umwelt* is key to unraveling the secrets of animal-fungi interactions, showing us how critter detectives navigate using their unique senses through the hidden kingdom of mushrooms.

Understanding an animal's *umwelt* isn't just a cool intellectual exercise; the term opens our eyes to the astonishing diversity and complexity of life on Earth. It helps us appreciate how a spider's web is not just a sticky trap, but a shimmering tapestry of vibrations guiding its every move. *Umwelt* shows us how a bat's echolocation paints a detailed picture of its surroundings in a symphony of sound. When we understand *umwelt*, we develop a greater appreciation for the complex interactions of life happening around us. Each species, with its unique sensory toolkit, contributes to the grand tapestry of our planet. Curious about the mysterious domains animals perceive? I recommend Ed Yong's book *An Immense World: How Animals Sense the Hidden Realms Around Us* and prepare to have your senses awakened!

Symbiosis in Shadows: Animal-Fungi Partnerships, the Good, the Bad, and the Ugly

Animals and fungi, unlikely partners, engage in a high-stakes game of give-and-take, forging alliances, trading resources, and occasionally throwing the occasional punch. This is the story of **symbiosis**, a fundamental ecological concept, describing the interaction between two different organisms living in close physical association. Partnerships between animals and fungi often involve negotiating deals, swapping resources, and, let's be honest, sometimes getting into a bit of a scuffle. Symbiosis can be a sweet deal, a raw deal, or just a 'meh' deal, depending on who you ask.

Have you ever thought about mole latrines? If not, beneath the forest floor, a vibrant example of **mutualism** unfolds. It is a three-way partnership between moles, *Hebeloma* mushrooms, and towering trees. Moles, members of order Eulipotyphla, which includes shrews and hedgehogs, inhabit underground burrows. Moles create nutrient-rich latrine deposits that serve as food for *Hebeloma* fungi. In return, the mushrooms' hyphae, acting as nature's sanitation crew, decompose the waste, preventing disease and creating a cleaner environment for the moles. The fungi, in return, form an intricate mycorrhizal network with nearby tree roots, shuttling these vital nutrients upwards while receiving sugars in return. This "you scratch my back, I'll scratch yours" showcases the survival benefits of mutually beneficial relationships.

Although I gravitated toward those feel-good, win-win mutualistic relationships, we can't ignore the rest of the crew. After all, symbiotic partnerships can have their complexities. For example, there's **commensalism**, the ultimate one-sided friendship. Imagine a dung fungus throwing a party on a pile of, well, you know. The herbivore who produced said pile? Completely oblivious, just going about its day. The fungus is having a blast, breaking down nutrients and contributing to the ecosystem, while the herbivore is just . . . there, not the least bit bothered.

But not all symbiotic relationships are unicorns and rainbows. **Predation** reminds us that nature can be a bit of a brutal business. Lurking beneath the decaying wood is the oyster mushroom, as much a predator as a jaguar in the Amazonian jungle. Imagine a nematode worm wriggling through the damp earth, suddenly ensnared by the mushroom's deadly traps. The fungus releases potent enzymes, dissolving the worm's body, transforming it into a nutrient-rich meal.

Now, let's talk about the toxic freeloaders. **Parasitism**. Perhaps the most gruesome example is the *Cordyceps* fungus that turns insects into zombies. Imagine an ant, the doomed **host**, going about its daily routine, suddenly infected by the fungal spores. The fungus infiltrates the ant's body, hijacking its nervous system, turning it into a puppet. The ant is compelled to climb to a high point, where the fungus erupts, releasing its spores to infect new victims. Parasitism is a chilling reminder of how the *Ophiocordyceps* fungus benefits at the cost of the ant's life.

I wrote this book to bring more light into the critical relationship between animals and fungi and its importance to sustaining our planet. Given the abundance of animal mycophiles, I will highlight a selection of representatives from different taxa and a common theme to showcase their connection with fungi.

Our journey begins with a focus on mutualism, where both animal and fungus gain from their partnership. We'll explore examples of commensalism, where one party reaps the rewards while the other remains unaffected. While parasitic relationships also exist, their complexities deserve a dedicated exploration. For now, we'll stay on the ground, focusing on the diverse inhabitants of our terrestrial world. From the tiniest nematode to the majestic elephant, each animal interacts with fungi in unique ways.

To navigate this hidden world, picture yourself equipped with a multitude of senses, such as compound eyes, antenna, and specialized scent detector as you embark on a journey through the realm of animals that consume, farm, and seek medicinal and psychedelic fungi. We'll explore the surprising diversity of animal mycophiles, representing both invertebrates (creatures without backbones) and vertebrates (those with a backbone). From the intricate webs of fungal-farming ants to the truffle-loving boar, we'll discover a world where every bite, every burrow, and every scent tells a story of interconnectedness.

So, get ready to activate your inner explorer. Join me on a journey into the realm of animal mycophiles, where the unseen becomes the extraordinary and the ground beneath our feet becomes a stage for a silent symphony of life.

Chapter 1

Opening up a Can of Worms

Unveiling the Secrets of Worms and Fungi

Let's dive into a world that wriggles and squirms, where myths of monstrous serpents intertwine with the humble realities of earthworms tilling our gardens. Forget dusty classifications and archaic labels—this is a journey celebrating the "wormy" essence that transcends mere taxonomy. We are talking about morphology rather than a specific classification category.

Worms are indeed a curious thing. The word "worm" originated from the Old Norse, *orm*, and Old English, *wyrm*, which means "serpent" or "dragon." World mythology and literature had many meanings for "worm". According to Viking mythology, the Midgard's Worm, a massive serpent, lay dormant at the depths of the ocean until Thor killed it. England whispers of a fearsome serpent cloaked in myths and called the "worm." These myths describe how the worm causes immense destruction. Science fiction and fantasy writers love to use the term "worm" as a fantasy creature; for example Frank Herbert's *Dune* features a giant sandworm, while the movie *Tremors* features creatures called Graboids, based on the legend of the Mongolian Death worm. Most likely the legendary cryptid was a lizard, genus *Amphisbaena*. Similar to snakes, we can deem anything without appendages for movement wormlike.

Today, when we mention the word, "worms" many images conjure up, from flatworms, roundworms, parasites, earthworms, maggots, and even other insect larvae such as mealworms. My focus will be on the major "wormy" critters. I will not discuss Phylum Platyhelminthes (the flatworms). Although there has been some evidence of fungi found in free-living flatworm guts, it's most likely from the flatworm's prey, rather than actual feasting on fungi. Let's embark on a respectful exploration of wormy critters, that is, all critters more advanced than flatworms.

We'll begin by examining the wriggling mysteries of the worm world, Nematoda and Annelida, and their fungal alliances. But our journey wouldn't be complete without some masqueraders! Maggots and mealworms, though not true worms, share the "wormy" stage, showcasing the diverse adaptations of the insect world. Their wriggling forms and voracious appetites play crucial roles in decomposition and waste recycling, reminding us that even the unpleasant can serve a vital purpose.

As we explore their world, we'll uncover the science of worms and the interconnectedness of life, the beauty in the seemingly insignificant, and the hidden magic in the soil beneath us.

Nematodes

*If all the matter in the universe except the
nematodes were swept away, our world would still
be dimly recognizable.*
—NATHAN COBB (Father of Nematology)

May I intrigue you with the nematodes, also known as the roundworms, with tales of tiny terrors that lurk within us and threaten our furry companions? As a survivor of a bout with parasitic *Ascaris* roundworms, I can attest to having a close encounter with such a nemesis. And I wasn't the only one harboring roundworm tenants—these parasites infect one billion people with at least one type of roundworm. But forget preconceptions of slimy, parasitic worms. Here we're celebrating the enigmatic "wormy" essence that defines the phylum Nematoda named after the Greek word *nemos*, meaning thread. My focus is on free-living nematodes thriving in the teeming world of soil, where they share space with fungi.

Most people can go a lifetime without ever seeing nematodes. Amongst all the animals I will discuss; nematodes have the most minimalist body plan, a tiny house with a big punch. Nematodes are normally microscopic. Their body form is cylindrical, hence their common name, roundworms. In front is the head with the mouth and at the rear is the tail containing the reproductive organs and the anus. Sexes are separate, meaning they are females or males, however, a few are hermaphroditic. They don't have segments, which makes them different from earthworms and insect larvae, and they sport a cuticle containing chitin that covers their body. Nematodes can be found in various habitats, including Polar Regions. They are tough. They can survive extreme conditions like deserts, tundra, and even the harsh vacuum of space. Nematodes proved to be a great candidate as test animals for experiments in space. In fact, the only survivors from the Columbia Space shuttle 2003 disaster were *C. elegans*, a common nematode. These tiny titans, outnumbering humanity with a staggering 28,000 species and 60 billion individuals per human, are the rulers of the underworld, weaving intricate relationships with the fungal kingdom.

In terms of soil ecology, nematodes and fungi have a mutually beneficial relationship. These nematodes live in the soil around the mycelium, and they feed on bacteria and other microorganisms. The nematodes release nutrients and enzymes that benefit the mushrooms. Together they break down organic material and recycle nutrients vital to the health of the ecosystem. Understanding the interactions between roundworms and fungi is important for managing mushroom cultivation and conserving biodiversity in natural ecosystems.

But beware, nematodes can be a double-edged sword. While some champion the cause of humanity by devouring mosquito larvae, others turn their voracious appetites towards our beloved mushrooms. Their relentless munching on fruiting bodies and mycelia can wreak havoc on mushroom farms, causing significant economic damage. Fungi often fight back, by unleashing a potent counter-attack against their microscopic foes, the nematodes. Imagine them launching a barrage of sticky traps that snag unsuspecting nematodes like flypaper, dooming them to become a fungal feast. Fortunately, nematodes have predators such as other nematodes, insect larvae, tardigrades, centipedes, mites, and even oyster mushrooms that hunt them as food.

Enter the oyster mushroom, *Pleurotus ostreatus,* a wood-rotting fungi with an appetite for nitrogen. When nematodes wander too close, they become prime targets for a source of nitrogen. Forget fangs or claws—this fungus wields filaments laced with poison, deftly spearing unsuspecting victims. By blocking the biochemical calcium gates, the poison induces paralysis and eventual death in the nematode. With a flick of its filament spear, the oyster injects a paralyzing toxin, transforming the nematode into a roundworm "slurpy," its nutrients absorbed.

Fungi and nematodes often have various relationships. Sometimes, they work together, other times they ignore each other. In commensalism, one organism benefits while the other is not affected. One interesting example of a commensalism relationship is that of *Pilobolus crystallinus*, the Dung Cannon fungi and the lungworm nematode genus *Dictyocaulus*. The lungworm benefits but no harm is done to the fungus. *Pilobolus* is important because it breaks down herbivore dung and recycles nutrients. *Pilobolus* has an amazing propelling mechanism for shooting out its spores, by producing fluid-filled vesicles containing a spore packet. They expel spores in a burst of fluid, the idea to spread spores as far as possible. We are talking about average speeds up to 16 meters per second (56 miles per hour) and a distance of 2.5 meters (8.2 feet). The lungworm takes advantage of this fungal rocket ship.

Ejected fungal spores, harboring the lungworm larvae like stowaways, trigger a domino effect of infection among grazing animals, jeopardizing the rancher's livelihood and the health of their herd. The lungworm nematode eggs hatch in the lungs and the larvae cause parasitic bronchitis. Cows cough the mucus filled with larvae out and then ingest them from grass or vegetation. After re-ingesting the larvae, the cows' digestive system processes them and eliminates them in the feces. Most grazing animals give fecal matter a wide berth, leaving the immobile larvae stranded and unable to spread. However, the larvae wriggle through the fluid-filled vesicle of the sporangium and wait for *Pilobolus'* explosive launch. The launch of the spores and the hitchhiking larvae guarantees greater dispersal and hence a better chance for the nematode to be consumed, continuing the cycle of infection. I offer my sincerest apologies to the bovine community if this proves unsettling.

Earthworms
Farmer's Friend and Fungi's Partner

The sun's rays dance through the canopy, creating a pattern of golden spots on the ground, while a small creature squirms into sight. It's an earthworm, not just any worm, but a champion of the Phylum Annelida, a diverse taxon boasting over 22,000 segmented species! These ringed marvels (*annellus*, in Latin, means "little ring") flaunt their long bodies, each segment separated by external annuli and internal septa. Earthworms are nature's ultimate soil superheroes. They drill deep tunnels, aerating the earth like tiny rototillers, letting water whoosh through and air fill the spaces, giving roots room to grow. Earthworms also break down organic matter, increasing the surface area for microbial activity and enhancing the nutrient cycling.

But earthworms aren't solo acts. They team up with saprobic fungi, nature's decomposers that break down dead matter into simpler compounds. Together, they recycle nutrients and contribute to the formation of rich humus.

Mycorrhizal fungi establish symbiotic relationships with plants, aiding in nutrient absorption and moisture retention from the soil while receiving sugars from the plants. Along with earthworms, the fungi aid in facilitating the colonization of plant roots by mycorrhizal enhancing nutrient cycling and enriching the soil. In return, earthworms transport fungal spores, spreading them around like tiny spore taxis, helping fungi colonize new areas and spreading soil fertility.

Fungi also provide a food source for earthworms in nutrient-poor soils, keeping the soil fueled up. Want to attract earthworms and their fungal pals? Add some compost with fungi to your soil—it's like an all-you-can-eat buffet for these soil superheroes! Not only will earthworms love your compost, but they will even eat toxic fungi with no problem. Earthworms have built-in super-detoxifiers that render poisons harmless. Talk about tough constitution!

So, the next time you see an earthworm wiggle by, remember: it's not just a worm, it's a living soil doctor with a team of fungal partners. Team earthworm/fungi are the friends of farmers and gardeners, and the secret to healthy, vibrant soil bursting with life. Show your support for these wiggly wonders! They're the unsung heroes of the garden, keeping the soil healthy and happy. One wiggle at a time.

Maggots: Insect Larvae

Meet the maggots, fly larvae often mistaken for worms. They play a starring role in the grand scheme of mushroom life. Many insects, like flies, butterflies, and beetles, go through a dramatic transformation called metamorphosis, spending part of their lives as munching larvae. Segmented bodies and hard shells shield these larvae, classifying them as insects within the arthropod kingdom.

Fungal gnats, for example, deposit their eggs right on the spongy caps. Long and limbless, these larvae slither and twist like living spaghetti, sharing their *vermiform* (worm-like form) with a staggering 75% of their insect kin!

To unlock the secrets of these 4,500-plus maggot-laying gnat species, let's peek into their life cycle. Flies, those buzzing insects we all know, are the grown-up versions of larvae. And while "worms" might send shivers down our human spines, with visions of contamination and parasites, the good news is that maggots in mushrooms rarely pose any real threat to us. Think of them as a tiny sprinkle of extra protein. By accident, we often munch on larvae in our fruits and veggies, and the same goes for those wild mushrooms we find in the woods.

Maggots are amazing eaters. Their mouths, equipped with sharp hooks, scrape and shred both the delicate mycelium network and the fleshy, fruiting bodies. Rough-textured skin further abrades the fungi, preparing a delectable feast. But their culinary prowess doesn't stop there. Maggots secrete enzymes that liquefy the fungal flesh, transforming it into a nutritious smoothie, readily slurped up and digested. Mycophagy at its best. The larvae that eat fungi play a vital role in the ecosystem, and we should not underestimate their importance. These wriggling larvae devour and dismantle organic matter, a key act in the grand play of decomposition. This breakdown process isn't just a tidy cleanup; it's a nutrient-recycling activity, ensuring the ecosystem's health and balance.

Some larvae have developed unique mutualistic relationships with certain fungi. For example, specific species of insects rely on fungi to provide them with essential nutrients or even act as nurseries for their larvae. In fact, larvae pay it back by being acrobats of spore dispersal, carrying fungal spores on their bodies and within their digestive systems. This art of zoochory allows fungi to colonize diverse landscapes. By consuming fungi, the larvae facilitate these mutualistic relationships, playing a crucial role in maintaining biodiversity and ecological stability. The larvae that feed on fungi are not just quirky little creatures that ruin your mushroom meal, but key players in the intricate web of life.

Besides nutrient cycling and spore dispersal, maggots are a vital food source for countless creatures, from birds and reptiles to amphibians and small mammals. They're a crucial link in the food web, ensuring energy flows from fungi to higher trophic levels. By supporting the fungi-munching larvae populations, these insects contribute to the survival and well-being of many other species in the ecosystem.

Mushroom lovers, rejoice! But be warned, nature's munchkins, the maggots and worms, are fierce competitors for your prized fungi. Cultivators, wield your sterile weapons—nematodes, yeast, and larvae tremble before your sterile techniques. Foragers, sharpen your eyes so you can reach those treasures before the wriggling feast begins. The early forager catches her mushroom before the worms do. But fret not, a little wiggle might just mean a thriving ecosystem. Remember, a bit of extra protein (courtesy of a stray maggot) is just nature's bonus seasoning, so, embrace reality, respect the animal mycophiles, and enjoy the abundance of the mushroom kingdom!

Chapter 2

Slow, Slimy, Snails

*For observing nature, the best
pace is a snail's pace.*
~Edwin Way Teale

Mollusk Mycophagy

The most common image of animals interacting with fungi often involves a snail munching on a mushroom. These slowpokes aren't just posing for the camera; they're playing a crucial role with the fungi they munch on. Terrestrial snails play a vital role in zoochory because of their preference for consuming fungal fruiting bodies. Snails and slugs belong to the Mollusca Phylum, a fascinating group of invertebrates showcasing various adaptations, almost like superpowers. Knowing a bit about their biology will help you understand their niche and interactions with fungi.

One defining feature mollusks share is the mantle—a unique thin, fleshy tissue enveloping the soft bodies of mollusks like snails, clams, squids, and octopuses. The mantle functions vary depending on the mollusk class. Specialized cells in the mantle, called the mantle epithelium, build the shell. They secrete calcium carbonate or proteins, determined by the species, layer upon layer, crafting a unique and protective armor. This continuous process allows the mollusk to grow and repair damage, ensuring its fortress remains strong.

The mantle acts as the mollusk's lungs. In aquatic species, it houses blood vessels or gills that extract oxygen from the water. Terrestrial mollusks rely on the mantle to absorb air from the environment. The mantle cavity, a space created by its inner folds, facilitates this gas exchange, ensuring efficient respiration. Their breathing is as fresh as a clam's (pun intended).

For some mollusks, like clams and scallops, the mantle is not just a passive structure. Its muscular fibers can contract and expand, allowing the animal to open and close its shell. This movement serves various purposes, from locomotion and feeding to protection from predators. In cephalopods, the internal mantle plays a crucial role in their jet-propelled movements.

But wait, there's more! The mantle is not just about physicality. Sensory cells embedded within its surface act as a touch receptor, detecting environmental cues like water pressure and chemical signals. This sensory awareness plays a vital role in the mollusk's behavior and survival. Welcome to the snail's *umwelt*.

Finally, the mantle contributes to waste removal, aiding in the elimination of byproducts from the mollusk's body. This helps maintain a healthy internal environment. While some mantle functions remain consistent across all mollusks, others adapt to fit the unique ecological niches and evolutionary paths of each species.

Gastropods: Fungal Eaters of the Forest

While terrestrial snails and slugs dominate the mycophagy spotlight, let's not forget their marine counterparts. Nudibranchs, those flamboyant sea slugs, are often predatory, but some, like the *Tambja*, have a taste for fungi. And then there's the marine snail *Bulla gouldiana*, which can grind both algae and fungus like a microscopic food processor. Even weirder? Certain marine gastropods indirectly consume fungi by feeding on organisms that have either feasted on or have a symbiotic relationship with fungi. For instance, let's consider the sea hare *Dolabella auricularia*. It consumes red algae that contains fungal spores. As a result, it gets nutrients from the fungi. Although the consumption of fungi by marine snails and nudibranchs remains less explored, there's interesting evidence suggesting fungi play a pivotal role in their diets and ecological dynamics. Unseen and silent, lurking in the ocean depths, marine fungi beckon for deeper scientific exploration.

Now let's turn our attention to terrestrial snails and slugs and their amazing anatomy. First things first, snails and slugs are the sloths of the mollusk world. They take life at a leisurely pace. Gastropoda means stomach foot, describing its mode of locomotion. Try crawling on your stomach. After a severe case of rug burn, you will learn to appreciate the snail.

The snail's body divides into three main sections: the head-foot, the visceral mass, and the mantle. The head-foot houses sensory organs, the mouth, and a muscular foot crucial for locomotion. Sporting a pair of tentacles atop their head, snails use these for touch, taste, and as homes for their light-and-dark-sensing eyes, unable to discern detailed images. Within the visceral mass reside the digestive, respiratory, and reproductive organs, featuring a mouth, pharynx, esophagus, stomach, and intestine. Waste exits via the anus post-digestion. The respiratory system involves a network of blood vessels facilitating gas exchange with the environment, with hemoglobin transporting oxygen throughout the body, absorbed through the skin. As mentioned earlier, the mantle secretes calcium carbonate, crafting the snail's coiled shell, and as the snail grows, the mantle adds layer upon layer, crafting that beautiful spiral home.

Slugs mirror snail anatomy but without the shell. The shell acts as a survival asset for terrestrial snails, providing organ support and safeguarding against predators and environmental elements. In moments of peril, snails retract into their shells for added protection, a luxury absent in slugs, making them more discreet. Slugs are well-suited to damp habitats, such as under rocks, near moss, or in moist gardens, where they thrive in low light or nocturnal conditions, while snails are more active during daylight. In mushroom hunting ventures, we often encounter slugs in damp environs, sharing a habitat preference with fungi. Dietary preferences set snails as herbivores and slugs as omnivores, encompassing plants, carrion, and fungi. Like culinary detectives, both sniff out their hidden targets, combing the undergrowth for the perfect fungal prize.

The snail/slug boasts two superpowers: the radula and slime. Behold the incredible radula, akin to a tongue armed with rows of teeth, adept at scraping and grinding food like leaves or fungi. The radula adapt to different food preferences, morphing into a grazing tool for mycophagy—a versatile "tongue" and weed-raker, suited for indulging in mushrooms. The radula features sharp, hooked teeth known as denticles for scraping while grazing, akin to a snail's Swiss Army knife, albeit with more drool. While mushroom hunting, you might observe the tattered remains of snail grazing, as evidenced by the teeth-like marks left by the radula. This tool is useful for identifying species. Each radula design is as unique as a snowflake.

Their second superpower? Slime for locomotion. Animals exhibit diverse locomotion methods, from sprinting like cheetahs to jumping like kangaroos. Snails and slugs generate their own mucous or slime to aid movement, akin to sliding on a self-made water slide. Walk outside on a sidewalk, in your garden, or even on your windowsill and you may observe the slime trail of a snail. In her book *Slime, A Natural History*, author Susanne Wedlich spends a chapter on the ubiquitous slime of the snail. According to Susanne Wedlich: "This kind of crawling is called viscoelasticity on an intermediate level, and snails have perfected the method by generating their own surf, allowing them to ride the waves in slow motion." Though sluggish, this type of locomotion requires a third of the snail's total energy. The production cost of slime varies depending on environmental factors such as temperature, humidity, and the snail's health. Susanne Wedlich further explains that snail slime serves not only as locomotion but also as a communication tool for finding sexual partners, conveying information about species, direction, and attractiveness—a stark contrast to human dating cues. I suppose a running nose in humans is a sure sign of not having optimal health or even some disease to avoid. Not for snails, apparently.

Gastropod mycophagy is a fascinating area necessitating further exploration to comprehend their role in fungal spore dispersal. Snails and slugs are like truffle-hunting pigs in the fungal world, sniffing out hidden treasures and leaving a trail of spores in their wake. They have discerning palates, some preferring the delicate chanterelles, while others are adventurous foodies, trying every mushroom that crosses their path. And don't worry about them getting poisoned—snails/slugs developed diverse defense mechanisms to steer clear of toxic compounds that prove lethal to other organisms. These mechanisms include behavioral, physiological, and biochemical adaptations.

Behavioral adaptations stand as the primary defense mechanism of snails against poisonous mushrooms. Snails are selective in their feeding behavior, preferring certain types of vegetation over others. This selectivity allows them to avoid consuming mushrooms that are poisonous. Remarkably, certain snail species showcase a learning ability, favoring non-toxic mushrooms after consuming toxic ones, hinting at their capacity to avoid particular mushroom types based on past encounters.

Physiological adaptations also come into play, contributing to snails' resistance against poisonous mushrooms. Studies propose snails neutralize toxic mushroom compounds by metabolizing them into less harmful forms. For instance, enzymes like glutathione transferases found in snails aid in detoxifying these toxic compounds. Biochemical adaptations are evident, as some snail species produce mucus containing defensive compounds such as alkaloids, shielding them not only from the toxic effects of mushrooms but also from predators and pathogens. A personal protective force field made of goo.

The snail/slug enjoys a tasty fungal meal and, in return, the mushroom benefits from the gastropod's spore dispersal. Snails and slugs are crucial players in fungal dispersal, acting as delivery drivers for the invisible world of spores. Think of their guts as tiny spore buses. When they chow down on mushrooms, those microscopic spores hitch a ride through their digestive system. And voilà: poop with a purpose! Snails, nature's messy carriers, deliver spore-sprinkled surprises—each one a potential habitat for future fungi.

In fact, scientists have caught these slimy couriers red-handed! One study found that omnivorous slugs carry a variety of *basidiospores* (mushroom spores) in their droppings, spreading them far and wide. Another study revealed that slugs, for example, *Deroceras invadens*, effectively dispersed *Tuber* (truffle) spores, emphasizing their role in mycorrhizal colonization of these precious gems.

But snails and slugs aren't just mushroom Johnny Appleseed devotees. One study showed snails acting as mini-taxis for lichen, helping them spread and expand their colonies. They're also delivery guys for slime molds, those weird and wonderful life forms often mistaken for fungi. Slime molds belong to the Kingdom Protista, the Class Myxomycetes, and they play a role in decomposing plants and feeding on fungal spores. Like fungi, they help in the recycling of nutrients.

So, the next time you see a snail slithering on your sidewalk, give it a nod of respect. This slimy superhero is playing a vital role in keeping our ecosystems healthy and diverse.

P.S.: Scientists are still uncovering the full extent of this slimy partnership, especially between snails and a special type of fungi called *arbuscular mycorrhizae*. These fungi form a vital network underground, connecting plants and helping them share nutrients.

These findings underscore the significant role of snails and slugs in fungal spore dispersal, showcasing their contribution to maintaining fungal diversity and ecosystem dynamics. Conducting further research, especially in relation to snails and arbuscular fungi, is imperative for a comprehensive understanding of their contributions.

Chapter 3

A Buzz about Flies and Other Fungi-Loving Arthropods

*Flies are not filthy . . . they are always
cleaning themselves,*

~ERICA McALISTER
(Curator of Diptera,
Natural History Museum, London)

Flies rock in dispersing fungal spores. In fact, many mushrooms such as stinkhorns do their best to attract not only flies but other insects. From their buzzing wings to their foot-tasting adventures, flies are fascinating creatures, even if they're not welcome guests during our mushroom hunts. Let's buzz through the biology of flies. Those pesky little winged daredevils that make a beeline for your food have quite an interesting biology. They belong to the insect order Diptera, a name derived from the Greek words *di* meaning two and *ptera* meaning "wings." Yep, flies have only two wings, and they have some serious flight skills.

They can zip around like miniature fighter jets, performing maneuvers that would make *Top Gun* pilots green with envy. And it's all thanks to their intricate wings. These wings beat at an astonishing rate of 200 to 600 times per second, creating the famous buzz we all know.

But let's not forget about their fabulous eyes. Flies have these massive, bulging compound eyes that cover most of their heads. It's like they're wearing fly-sized VR goggles. These eyes give them a panoramic view of the world, which comes in handy when they're trying to find an available tasty mushroom or evade a pesky fly swatter. Now, here's a fun fact: flies have taste buds on their feet. Flies on your sandwich aren't just sightseeing, they are sampling the goods. Talk about having a foot fetish for food!

And we can't talk about flies without mentioning their remarkable ability to reproduce. Flies are notorious for their speedy breeding habits. They can go from egg to adult in as little as seven days. It's a race to see who can mature the fastest. As mentioned earlier, fly larvae love to munch on mushrooms. Imagine seeing flies and larvae feasting on your edible mushroom. For the forager, it's always a racing game, getting to the mushroom before the maggots do.

Eggs laid by female flies hatch in these materials, giving rise to maggots that thrive on the organic matter, including the mycelium and developing mushrooms. In moments, the fly larvae turn the fungi into mushroom shakes.

Yet no one is more annoyed with flies than the mushroom cultivator. Flies can be significant pests on mushroom farms because of their ability to cause damage to the mushrooms and disrupt the overall growth and production process. Who can blame them? Mushrooms' delicious bounty beckons nearby flies, drawing them in like magnets.

This feeding activity can lead to significant crop loss and contamination. Flies can transfer pathogens to mushrooms, causing infections and diseases. Buzzing invaders! Pesky flies infiltrate the farm, resulting in severe damage to the crop and reduced yield and quality. Contaminated mushrooms are not only unsuitable for sale but can also pose health risks to consumers. Mushroom farms require specific conditions of temperature, humidity, and airflow to promote proper growth. Flies can disrupt these conditions. Again, the emphasis of this book is on the mutualistic relationship between flies and fungi, but knowing this relationship can help the hapless mushroom cultivator. This section dives into the captivating world of fly-fungus cooperation, but its lessons go beyond. Mushroom growers of all levels can unlock solutions through its knowledge.

Fungal gnats, belonging to the family Sciaridae, are a prime example of mutualism because of their crucial role in fungal spore dispersal. You can find these tiny flies in both indoor and outdoor environments. The larvae feed on decaying organic matter, including decomposing mushrooms. As they chomp and burrow, these larvae gather a hitchhiking cargo: mushroom spores clinging to their squirming bodies. These spores get whisked away to new locations, finding fertile ground to start a new fungal colony. But wait, there's more! These larvae don't just snack on decomposing mushrooms: they also dine on the mycelium, the network of fine, thread-like structures that make up the vegetative body of fungi. The larvae thrive on the nutrient-rich fungi, which contribute to their growth and development. While the symbiotic relationship between fungal gnats and mushrooms is beneficial, as stated earlier, the larvae of fungal gnats can pose a risk to cultivated mushrooms by consuming their mycelium. This can cause significant damage to commercial mushroom crops.

Like the adult flies, when the larvae move to new locations, either by crawling or being carried by the wind or other means, they transport the spores to different areas, facilitating the spread and colonization of mushrooms. Fungal gnats help in the breakdown and decomposition of organic matter, including plant debris and decaying mushrooms. By consuming and breaking down these materials, they contribute to the recycling of nutrients in the ecosystem. Plants and other organisms can then take the nutrients released through decomposition up, promoting a healthy nutrient cycle.

The Funky Fungus Flies Love: A Tale of Stinkhorns and Spores

Imagine a mushroom that looks like a neon orange party horn and smells like your gym socks after a grueling workout. I have to be honest, the first time I spotted a stinkhorn, it looked like the monstrous appendage of some slumbering subterranean beast. I identified it as a *Phallus impudicus* by name, thrusting its, uh, unique form skyward. To clarify, many species of stinkhorns do not resemble phalluses. Once considered disgusting by polite society, *Phallus impudicus* will serve as our example of a classical stinkhorn. Beatrix Potter, the beloved children's author and mycologist, was so revolted by its appearance that she never painted it, as she did so many other mushrooms. Charles Darwin's daughter Etty eradicated stinkhorns from their surrounding areas in case it corrupted the morals of her maids. In fact, because of its stench, Victorians, ever the sticklers for decorum, blamed the stinkhorn for everything from plagues to poltergeists.

While notorious for their nose-pinching aroma, stinkhorns, which are all saprobes, surprise with their diversity of shapes and sizes. The classic stinkhorn, *Phallus impudicus*, like a mischievous jester, erupts from its egg-like disguise, revealing a crimson stalk topped with a putrid olive-green cap. The dog stinkhorn, *Mutinus caninus*, prefers a more subtle approach, resembling a, well, let's just say, a very specific part of a canine anatomy. It may not be the most elegant stinkhorn, but its unique shape will spark conversation (and maybe a few giggles).

But not all stinkhorns are flamboyant exhibitionists. The lattice stinkhorn, or red cage fungus *Clathrus ruber*, takes things up a notch, transforming into a delicate scarlet sculpture, its intricate arms reaching out to form a macabre cage. Rotting meat? Anyone? Amidst the forest floor, *Clathrus archeri*, the octopus stinkhorn's slender tentacles, twist and writhe, their sway mimicking an underwater creature. Lacking pageant-worthy looks, its grotesque figure grabs attention (and might churn your stomach). If you're looking for something outlandish, the columned stinkhorn, *Clathrus columnatus*, takes the cake (or should we say, the spore?). This architectural marvel boasts six crimson columns that intertwine to form a cage, sheltering a putrid green treasure within. It's a Gothic masterpiece gone bad, a testament to the bizarre creativity of nature.

And then there's the Starfish Fungus, aka the Anemone Stinkhorn! Its Latin name, *Aseroe rubra*, translates to "disgusting red juice," which hints at its unusual odor. Named by French botanist Jacques Labillardière in 1792, it became the first described native Australian fungus. Through hitchhiking on garden mulch and woodchips, the starfish fungus has achieved global distribution, earning widespread recognition from mycologists (and perhaps less enthusiastically from gardeners). Interestingly, it's even reached islands untouched by humans. This leads me to believe that long-distance flying animals might be the secret agents behind its impressive spread!

In fact, stinkhorns developed a fascinating strategy to ensure their spores spread far and wide. Unfurling their vibrant banners of decay, these slimy fungi from the Phallaceae family beckon flies with the promise of a putrid feast. The odor is thanks to a chemical cocktail of volatile organic compounds (VOCs), like dimethyl trisulfide (the same stuff that makes me cry when slicing onions), wafting through the air and attracting many insects to the convincing rot. Insects, with their sensitive sense of smell, can't resist this pungent perfume of decaying goodness. But the stinkhorn isn't just a smelly siren song. It also dresses to impress, sporting bright colors like red, orange, or yellow. This visual cue works like a neon flashing sign, guiding flies and other insects closer to the source of the aroma.

Once the flies land, they step on a sticky, gooey layer called the gleba, packed with millions of tiny spores just waiting to hitch a ride. The spores adhere to the bodies of the insects, often on their legs or other body parts. After leaving the stinkhorn mushroom, the flies continue their normal activities, carrying the attached spores with them. As they fly to different locations, they deposit the spores onto suitable substrates, such as decaying plant material or soil, where they have the potential to germinate and establish new fungal colonies. And voilà, a new generation of stinkhorn mushrooms sprouts, thanks to their odorous charm and fly-powered delivery service. This stinky partnership is a prime example of mutualism.

So next time you encounter a funky-smelling fungus in the woods, remember, it's not just nature being gross, it's a genius strategy playing out right before your eyes (and nose). And who knows, maybe you'll even spot a fly or two sporting a spore-covered mustache—a living testament to the fascinating world of stinkhorn mushrooms and their insect fans.

Can a mushroom get rid of pesky flies?

The legend of the Fly Agaric, *Amanita muscaria*, and its relationship to flies has always intrigued me. *Amanita muscaria* is the most identifiable mushroom in popular culture thanks to the Mario Brothers video game and it's the toadstool in Alice in Wonderland. The Fly Agaric emoji has become a trendy symbol on social media, and individuals are incorporating it into their clothing and artwork. The first mushroom species I learned and identified based on its rather obvious structure was *Amanita muscaria*. Derived from the Latin word *musca*, which

signifies "fly," the term *muscaria* denotes a specific species. The scientific name of the common housefly is *Musca
domestica*. Every name had a sensible explanation. Fly
Agaric's origin can be traced back to its use as a fly insec-
ticide, thanks to its ibotenic acid and muscimol content.
The recipe is simple: crumble up some *Amanita muscaria*
caps and place in saucers of milk. The toxic compounds
present in the mushroom intoxicate and kill the flies. But
beyond its aesthetic allure, this iconic mushroom boasts
a curious legend: its reputation as a fly-killing weapon.
Does science corroborate this folklore, or is it a whimsical
mushroom myth?

Amanita muscaria contains ibotenic acid, a water-
soluble toxin that, according to folklore, lures flies with
its enticing aroma before delivering a fatal dose. However,
research sheds fascinating light on the true fate of these
winged visitors. Is their death caused by the toxin or
drowning? Giorgio Samorini, in his book *Animal and
Psychedelics*, discovered that the collected flies were in a
drunken stupor, rather than dead. "If touched lightly with
a pencil, some will react by sluggishly moving their legs
while others remain unperturbed in their position. With
the help of a magnifying glass, it is possible to observe a
peristaltic movement of their bodies, however—clear
proof they are not dead. After a period of time that may
vary from thirty minutes to fifty hours, the flies wake
up." After a night of partying, the flies finally wake from
their inebriation and dart away. Imagine flies in a heady
stupor, limbs pulsating in slow-motion jigs, or drifting
into psychedelic naps in the cap's crimson milky pool.
They are not deceased, but amid a prolonged psychedelic
journey. In a manner reminiscent of someone recovering

from a night on the town, these flies eventually regain their faculties and fly off, buzzing away without a care in the world.

While flies don't meet their demise on the Fly Agaric, the toxins impair their nervous system, making them easy pickings for predators. A 2016 study by Lumpert and Kreft, "Catching flies with *Amanita muscaria*," highlights a fly swat may be all it takes to send these inebriated insects to an early, albeit less poetic, end.

The Fly Agaric's chemical cocktail, though not fatal to flies, leaves them inebriated and vulnerable. These woozy winged wanderers become easy pickings for predators. Nonetheless, flies visit the mushroom for various reasons, such as seeking food or shelter. Flies feed on decaying organic matter, including decomposing plant material and fungal fruiting bodies. *Amanita muscaria*, like other mushrooms, can attract flies by emitting volatile compounds that mimic the scent of decay. In return, flies ferry fungal spores to far-flung corners, spreading the magic of mushrooms across the land. It's no wonder why this iconic mushroom is not a dedicated fly-killer. The quirky world of ecological interactions reminds us the natural world is often stranger and more nuanced than our folklore suggests.

Arthropods Cannot resist Eating Fungi

If there is a Creator, he must have
an inordinate fondness for beetles.
~J.B.S. HALDANE

Beetle Fungimania

Beetles, a diverse group within the Phylum Arthropoda, make up a staggering 25% of all animal species. In the enchanting world of mycophagy, where fungi and animals form unique connections, beetles play a pivotal role. Boasting nearly 400,000 species, beetles hold the title for the largest and most diverse group of insects.

Bursting with over 3,500 species, the Pleasing Fungus Beetle family transforms fallen logs and mossy landscapes into vibrant galleries of red, orange, and black patterns, creating a dazzling spectacle in tropical regions. True to their mycophilic nature, these beetles relish the hyphae and spores of molds, mildews, and other fungi, found in damp environments. Their habitats range from wet pallets in warm buildings to sea containers with condensation, making them adaptable and widespread.

The importance of beetles in mycophagy extends beyond the pleasing fungus beetles. Species like the hairy fungus beetle, foreign grain beetle, plaster beetles, and minute fungus beetles contribute to the ecosystem's balance. They infest various environments, from warehouses with leaky roofs to dried mushrooms. Other beetles, alongside the obligate fungivore ambrosia beetles, also

44

play a crucial role in mycophagy and zoochory. Adding another layer to the intricate relationships between beetles and fungi in nature. *Triplax thoracica*, a species in the pleasing fungus beetle family, exhibits a strong fondness for Oyster (*Pleurotus*) mushrooms, with 98% of sightings occurring on these delectable fungi. Oyster mushrooms are saprobes, aiding in the decomposition of dying or dead wood.

Of all the fungus-loving beetles, one caught my attention. Let us look deep within the enchanted realm of fallen logs and gnarled trees, where moss carpets the ground and sunlight dribbles through leafy canopies. There we will witness the fierce competition, and an unlikely partnership forged in the realm of bracket mushrooms. This is the saga of the forked fungus beetle (*Bolitotherus cornutus*) a miniature knight clad in armored carapace, its life woven with bracket fungi. Built like a beetle-shaped tank, these creatures exhibit a dazzling sexual dimorphism. The males, with their gleaming forked antlers, strut through the fungal realm, resembling miniature *Triceratops*. Females, despite not having a forked appearance, adorn themselves in equally impressive armor.

At the heart of the forked fungus beetle's existence lies a gastronomic preference for the aged, robust bracket mushrooms, including the genera F*omitopsis, Ganoderma,* and *Ischnoderma*, found on weakened trees and fallen logs. Their affinity for *Ganoderma* fungi, especially *Ganoderma applanatum, G. tsugae,* and *G. lucidum*, becomes a stage for intriguing social behaviors. Horns lock, snouts jab, and a silent battle for dominance plays out on the surface of a prized *Ganoderma* conk. Vince Formica, a researcher at Swarthmore College, with an eye for the dramatic, has captured these clashes in his enthralling videos, forever preserving the fierce beauty of these nocturnal jousts.

Yet, these beetles are not just brawlers. Faced with danger, they unleash a secret weapon —a potent chemical cocktail brewed deep within their abdomens. This volatile elixir, deployed with remarkable timing, becomes a noxious shield, a testament to their adaptive resourcefulness. Another ploy in self-defense is playing dead, much like an opossum.

Daylight unveils evidence of their presence as small brown patches on *Ganoderma applanatum* conks, a result of females crafting nests, laying eggs, and covering them with frass (biological wastes), showcasing their nurturing instincts.

Upon hatching, the grub-like larvae begin a captivating journey of tunneling, deciding between the sheltered darkness of conks or venturing into the sunlight before burrowing. The key factor contributing to their remarkable longevity is the deliberate decision they make to inhabit a specific species of bracket fungi.

The intricate existence of the forked fungus beetle's life extends to its interactions with mites—legged, pink dots found on the beetle's head. These phoretic (hitchhiking) mites, originating from fungi, leverage the beetle's longer legs for mobility, offering a quirky yet integral aspect of the beetle's existence. The mites feed on fungi and fungal spores. A curious commensalism partnership that speaks volumes about the interconnectedness of this miniature ecosystem. Despite lacking studies, the beetle undoubtedly excels in dispersing spores.

The Forked Fungus Beetle's saga is not just a chronicle of individual lives; it's a vibrant thread of fungi, mites, and beetles, each playing their part in the grand performance. From the clash of horns to the muted dedication of a larval nursery, from the chemical warfare to the curious alliance with mites, this story beckons further exploration, inviting us to delve deeper into the intricate dynamics of life within a log infected with shelf fungi. So the next time you stumble upon a fallen tree, remember—beneath the bark, amidst the decaying wood, a vibrant drama unfolds, one where beetles rule, fungi provide the feast, and nature thrives.

The Hidden World of Flat Bugs: Connoisseurs of Mycelium Feasts

In the secretive realm beneath bark and within the decaying wood of our local forests, a fascinating insect thrives—the flat bug. In the family Aradidae, part of the Hemiptera group, these true bugs possess a unique set of features that make them both elusive and intriguing.

Imagine a miniature pancake of an insect, no bigger than a grain of rice, sandwiched between the bark and wood of a fallen tree. The world of the flat bug is a place where the creature is so flattened that it appears as if a tiny rolling pin pressed on it. These cryptic and elusive creatures, aptly named for their squashed bodies, belong to the family Aradidae and measure a mere 3 to 11 millimeters. Flat bugs skitter and hide under rocks, in the cracks of dead trees, or beneath loose bark.

What sets flat bugs apart are their hypodermic-needle-like mouthparts, resembling long beaks that function as straws. These stylets are thread-thin and longer than the flat bug's own body. With these precision instruments, flat bugs tap into the hidden veins of the forest: the mycelium.

The fungi's mycelium serves as the primary food for these cryptic insects. Thin, filamentous hyphae weave through the soil and decaying wood, composing the vast network of the mycelium. This adapted stylet, slurps up the fungi's nutrient-rich juices, savoring and siphoning life from the fungal. These masters of disguise have taken flatness to an extreme. Their wings, though present, remain small and tucked away, evidence of their preference for a hidden lifestyle. But flat bugs aren't all loners. They're social creatures, often found in clandestine gatherings under bark or amidst fallen logs. Despite their inconspicuous nature, flat bugs showcase a worldwide presence, with the most diverse species thriving in the vibrant landscapes of Australia. While many temperate species live under the bark of dead trees, tropical counterparts prefer leaf litter or fallen twigs and branches as their habitat.

The flat bug's life cycle is as secretive as their hideouts. Researchers have overlooked these creatures, deeming them insignificant because of their lack of economic threat and rarity as agricultural pests. However, their importance in the ecosystem lies in their mycophagous tendencies—feeding on the mycelia and fruiting bodies of wood-rotting fungi.

Flat bugs, often dismissed as mere shadows, evoke a sense of mystery and wonder, reminding us of the hidden realms teeming with untold stories and unseen wonders. These tiny enigmas navigate the labyrinthine mycelial maze with practiced ease, their flattened bodies gliding over tendrils like vehicles on an unseen road. The decomposing wood, infused with the mycelium's potent alchemy, becomes their bounty, fueling their survival and

providing evidence of the underrated diversity and ingenuity of the insect world.

Springtails: Tiny Acrobats with a Taste for Fungi

Have you ever inspected a mushroom, only to discover
tiny specks nestled within its intricate gills? Not flies,
larvae, or conventional insects, but the curious world of
springtails, also known as snow fleas. Despite their unassuming size, they're equipped with powerful appendages
called furculae. These forked structures act like springs,
launching springtails into the air with impressive force.
Imagine jumping 100 times your own height! Watching
these small creatures twist and turn in mid-air is a testament to their remarkable acrobatic abilities. While
springtails are famous for their jumping skills, we must
also acknowledge their other noteworthy qualities. They
come in a dazzling array of shapes and colors, from sleek
and elongated to plump and globular. A kaleidoscope of
color—white, black, purple, red, and orange - adorns the
bodies of springtails, with some featuring unique mottled
designs.

Springtails, though not insects, are intriguing creatures
that belong to the class Collembola within the subphylum
Hexapoda. Boasting 30 diverse families and a staggering
8,000 species worldwide, this class showcases the remarkable versatility of these tiny, oval, or elongated arthropods.
Despite their resemblance to insects with six legs, biologists argue springtails have a distinct lineage, marked by
unique traits. Sporting antennae, three pairs of legs, and
a segmented body, springtails exhibit a diverse array of

mouthparts, ranging from simple to highly specialized. One such feature is their internal chewing mechanism, a departure from insects with external chewing parts.

The furcula, a bi-forked appendage, and the collophore, a tube-like structure, contribute to the intricate anatomy and survival strategies of springtails. Mimicking grasshoppers or fleas, these creatures use their furcae as catapults, releasing them with explosive force to evade potential predators. The name "springtail" comes from their remarkable ability to jump, facilitated by their furcae—tiny spring-like appendages located under their bodies. The collophore plays a crucial role in their ability to attach to surfaces, preventing them from losing balance during takeoff and descent, allowing them to adhere to landing surfaces.

While sometimes mistaken for fleas, springtails stand out thanks to their round, soft bodies, a stark contrast to the dark brown, flattened form of true fleas. It is worth mentioning that springtails do not pose any threat to humans or pets, and they do not carry diseases or cause any harm to the structure of houses.

Springtails have a particular fondness for eating fungi. They munch on mold, spores, and even decaying plant matter, playing a crucial role in the decomposition process. But the relationship between springtails and fungi isn't always one-sided. Some fungi, like *Laccaria bicolor*, lure springtails close with their enticing scent, only to trap them and use them as a source of nitrogen. It's a fascinating twist in the hidden world of the forest floor.

Beyond their distinctive characteristics and dietary habits, springtails play a vital role in the ecosystem. As populations of springtails fluctuate in response to changes in temperature, moisture, and food availability, these inconspicuous insects thrive in environments rich in decaying leaves and humus.

Despite their small size, springtails play a vital role in returning valuable nutrients to the soil. They also aid in the spread of beneficial fungi that protect plants from diseases. So, the next time you see a flash of movement beneath a mushroom's cap, remember the important work that these tiny acrobats are doing behind the scenes.

Chapter 4

Social Insects: Industrial Mushroom Farmers

An ant is a wise creature for itself, but it is a shrewd thing, in an orchard or garden.
~Francis Bacon

For millennia, agriculture stood as humanity's crown jewel—the revolutionary leap from hunter-gatherer sustenance to settled abundance. Around 12,000 years ago, during the Neolithic Revolution, we traded precarious nomadic existence for permanent homesteads and cultivated fields, replacing the uncertainties of the hunt with the steady bounty of domesticated crops and livestock. Yet, in the realm of fungus farming, humans are mere newbies.

While our ancient ancestors foraged mushrooms from the wild, deliberate cultivation wouldn't bloom until 600 CE in China and Japan. Remarkably, this practice developed independently—not just in human minds, but also in the insect world. In fact, social insects hold the undisputed trophy in this arena, having pioneered myco-cultivation a staggering 60 million years ago. This ancient fungal-insect coevolution has captivated biologists. My exploration dives deep into three fascinating groups of social insects: leaf-cutting ants, mound-building termites, and ambrosia beetles—whose lives revolve around their cultivated fungi.

Unlike our sight-reliant dependence, these insects boast a dazzling array of sensory capabilities, fundamental to both their survival and social complexities. Sights, sounds, smells, tremors—the tapestry of their perception, their unique umwelt, allows them to interact with and navigate their ecological niches in ways we can only marvel at. Prepare to shed your human lens and enter their world, where fungal farms flourish in underground cathedrals and symbiotic activity unfolds in intricate social networks.

These creatures have developed specialized antennae equipped with receptors that can detect chemicals, a skill known as chemoreception. This ability lets them pick up on chemical signals in their environment, aiding in communication, finding food, recognizing their colony mates, and identifying potential dangers. Alongside this, they possess mechanoreception, which involves sensing physical stimuli through their legs and body. Tiny hairs on their legs act as touch sensors, feeling the world with a delicacy we can only dream of. They possess an innate ability to decipher the meaning behind every rustle of a leaf and vibration in the soil. They can discern textures, measure distances, and even sense minute changes in air pressure, helping them navigate treacherous terrain and build intricate underground tunnels.

Although their compound eyes lack the intricate clarity of ours, they perceive the world as a blend of motion and shade. Flashes and flickers provide enough information to guide them through foraging expeditions, escape predators, and recognize individuals within their colony.

Certain ants, termites, and beetles possess thermoreceptive abilities or temperature sensors. This helps them regulate their body heat and guides them to warm nesting spots or foraging, crucial for maintaining optimal body temperature in the ever-changing world. They can also sense the very moisture in the air with hygroreceptors, avoiding damp disaster zones and keeping their fungal gardens in perfect humidity. This ensures the survival of their entire colony and the delicate ecosystems they cultivate.

Even without hearing like mammals, insects can sense vibrations and airborne sounds through specialized sensory organs, aiding in communication and detecting dangers or resources. Some can even detect ultrasonic frequencies, inaudible to us but crucial for communication and predator avoidance. Research suggests that certain insects, including ants and termites, have magnetoreception, allowing them to detect the Earth's magnetic field. This internal compass allows them to navigate vast distances during foraging trips and maintain complex social structures within their colonies.

Overall, the sensory prowess of ants, termites, and beetles showcases nature's incredible adaptations. These social insects exhibit an almost AI-like ability to sense, thrive, and communicate within their intricate ecosystems. So the next time you see an ant marching by, take a moment to appreciate the silent symphony playing in its tiny head—a sensory feast that puts our high-tech gadgets to shame.

Leaf-Cutting Ants (Atta spp)

Ants, those pint-sized powerhouses, are like nature's tech-savvy engineers. Let's crack open their amazing anatomical toolbox and see what makes them tick! First off, let's explore the ant's head—it's their command center, housing a brain smaller than a sesame seed, yet mighty in orchestrating ant activities. Next, we have the ant's antennae, those delicate appendages that quiver and wiggle, functioning as their means of communication, comparable to an ant's Wi-Fi. The thorax of the ant is a powerhouse for its six small but strong legs. The sight of ants lifting objects many times their body weight is a testament to their incredible strength, making them the bodybuilders of the insect world. Observing ants might motivate you to join the gym for some serious muscle-building workout.

The abdomen is an ant's personal pantry, always stocked with goodies from their tireless foraging. But it's not just a grocery bag; some ants have secret weapons hidden up their sleeves—stingers! These prickly security systems keep unwanted guests at bay, ensuring their snack supply and colony members stay safe. Let's continue on with our mushroom farming leaf-cutter ants.

Imagine an ancient civilization thriving for over 30 million years, not on brute force, but on meticulous agriculture and coordinated teamwork. That's the reality of leaf-cutter ants, fascinating insects belonging to the genera *Atta* and *Acromyrmex*, with 47 known species. These industrious creatures cultivate their own "mushroom farms" within their nests, growing a special fungus that serves as their sole food source. Leaf-cutter ant colonies operate like organized machines, thanks to a specialized caste system. Each member plays a vital role in sustaining the colony's survival and prosperity. At the top of the ant hierarchy, we have the queen ant, who reigns supreme at the heart of the nest. Her sole purpose is to lay eggs, ensuring the colony's continued existence. Unlike the queen, male ants live a brief existence. Their primary goal is to mate with a queen and establish new colonies, after which they bid farewell to the world. While the queen gets all the glory, the colony thrives on the tireless work of its nannies (minims), field agents (minors and mediae), and security detail (majors).

Minims, the tiniest but essential workers, tend to the burgeoning brood and cultivate the fungus gardens, the colony's lifeblood. The size of the minors increases over the minims as they serve as security. They patrol foraging trails with unwavering vigilance, ready to repel any threat with their sharp mandibles. Mediae form the backbone of the colony's food supply chain. These medium-sized workers cut leaves and transport them back to the nest, providing the raw material for their fungal farms. Towering over their smaller kin, majors serve as the colony's armored knights. Equipped with formidable jaws and stingers, they defend the nest from intruders and clear obstacles from foraging trails.

Leaf-cutter ants thrive not just because of individual roles but from the flawless synergy forged through communication. They speak through an array of chemical signals known as pheromones, orchestrating their actions. Imagine tiny scent flags scattered across their intricate highways, guiding, warning, and uniting these meticulous farmers. Functioning as a chemical messenger, the Dufour's gland, nestled in the ant's abdomen, is the key element of their communication network. This gland, named for Swiss entomologist Léon Jean Marie Dufour, plays a crucial role in how ants interact. This gland crafts and emits Dufour's gland secretions, pivotal compounds steering various aspects of ant interaction. These chemicals aid in recognizing kin, marking trails, and signaling defense. One whiff might signal "kin here," another, a trail to juicy leaves, and another, a spine-tingling alarm of approaching danger. These scent bombs rouse the colony, summoning reinforcements or triggering desperate evacuations when faced with formidable threats.

However, leaf-cutters use more than just scent to communicate. Gentle touches transform into nudges and taps, as antennae explore and body postures convey significant messages. Even the ground vibrates with their unspoken conversations, transmitted through tiny tremors produced by stridulations, the rhythmic rubbing of body parts to produce sound. This intricate web of communication woven from scent, touch, and silent tremors, allows these social maestros to coordinate their complex lives. This is what fuels the incredible success of leaf-cutter ants, where individual roles intertwine into a harmonious existence.

Deep beneath the vibrant canopies of Central and South America, in the silent world of subterranean chambers, the leaf-cutting ants, skilled architects of the *Atta* and *Acromyrmex* genera, reign as nature's master cultivators. They tend to their most prized possession: a lush garden of fungus known as *Leucoagaricus gongylophorus*. It's worth mentioning that this species of fungus will only produce mushrooms when the ants desert their colony.

The ants haul leaf fragments to subterranean nests, transforming these chambers into lush "fungus gardens." Attentively, they curate these garden havens, mixing leaf bits with their waste to craft a nourishing compost for the fungus. With a keen eye on temperature and humidity, these ants micromanage these gardens, safeguarding them with antimicrobial secretions and eradicating pathogens. They also remove competing molds or pests to maintain the health of the cultivated fungus. In the safe environment, their larvae feast on the succulent fungal mycelium. It's a partnership at its best: the ants provide a consistent nutrient stream, while the fungus, adapted over eons, thrives within the ant colonies. This obligate mutualism, a bond so tight it defines their very existence, is a captivating chapter in the story of life. The fungus clings to the leaf-cutter ants, its survival intertwined with their every step, while the ants rely on its bountiful yields for their own sustenance. This intricate dependence is a window into the delicate web of life, a reminder of the profound dynamics of mutualistic symbiosis and the interdependencies that exist within ecosystems.

Cracking the Code of Cellulose: Termites & Their Outsourcing Fungal

Before delving into termites, let's draw a comparison with our first group of fungal farmers: ants. While termites may share some resemblance with ants, they possess distinct characteristics. Ants boast a narrow waist, granting them a segmented appearance. In contrast, termites feature a more uniform cylindrical body lacking a pronounced waistline. Their antennae differ—ants sport bent or angled antennae, whereas termites possess straight, bead-like ones. Wings serve as another differentiating factor: ants possess larger, tougher forewings compared to their hindwings, whereas termites have wings of equal size and texture. After mating, termites shed their wings, while ants typically retain theirs.

Similar to ants, termites exhibit an impressive social structure. At the summit of the termite hierarchy stands the termite queen, commanding a retinue of termite attendants to ensure the colony's continuous expansion. Both the queen and king, each equipped with wings, collaborate in mound construction. Despite the title, the king's primary role is akin to being the queen's consort, responsible for fertilizing eggs—the royal lineage's key contributor.

The worker termites, the unsung champions of the colony, toil day and night, maintaining the efficiency of their fungal farms. These individuals epitomize termite agriculture, nurturing their fungal yields with unwavering care. Remarkably, unlike most farmers, they don't lament pests decimating their crops; after all, they are the consumers!

Equipped as the colony's guardians, soldier termites resemble bouncers at an exclusive club, wielding formidable mandibles to fend off intruders with remarkable zeal. No uninvited guests breach their defenses! Last, we encounter the juvenile termites—the colony's future. Comparable to high school students, they learn the intricacies of termite society, destined to graduate into roles as workers, soldiers, or even future royalty. So, there you have it—the social order of fungus-growing termites in a nutshell.

Unlike leaf-cutter ants, the Termitidae family faces a daunting dietary dilemma: lignin, a molecule wall fortress, no insect can digest. But termites, these tiny titans of evolution, have found two ingenious ways to crack this code, splitting into two symbiotic relationships.

Termites have developed a clever strategy to consume wood by forming mutualistic relationships with symbiotic organisms that can break down lignin. In the vibrant jungles of the New World, termites flexed their biochemical muscles, crafting gut factories equipped with enzyme battering rams that smash cellulose into bite-sized sugars. But they didn't do it alone. They outsourced microscopic allies—bacteria and protozoa, their gutsy chefs, who whipped up a fermentation frenzy, turning wood pulp into a nutritious broth.

Across the ocean, in the sun-baked savannas of the Old World, a different dynasty emerged—the Macrotermitinae. Lacking the cellulose-digesting protozoa, these fungi fanatics took a different fork in the evolutionary road. They became mushroom farmers, cultivating *Termitomyces* fungi in meticulously manicured gardens within their towering mounds. Picture it: subterranean greenhouses brimming with fungal gardens, providing a smorgasbord for the termite colony. Now turn your attention to the main attraction—the African Mound building termite, *Macrotermes natalensis*.

Delving deeper into the termite's anatomy reveals a marvel of adaptation that fuels their fungal feast. These critters boast formidable mandibles, jaws so mighty, they could outmatch a wood chipper. They chomp away at the wood, turning it into manageable bits. As we venture down their bodies, we encounter their streamlined thorax, which allows for agile maneuvering in tight spaces, ensuring efficient delivery of wood to their fungal partners. Think of it as a sleek delivery truck, navigating the complex subterranean city with grace and purpose.

But wait, it gets even more functional when we reach their abdomen, or as I like to call it, the "fungus pantry." Here's where they stash their cherished fungal yields, nurturing them with meticulous care. Humidity levels, temperature and cleanliness are all well maintained. The delicate fungal combs, constructed inside the mound, provide the perfect platform for *Termitomyces* growth. Imagine a miniature greenhouse, constantly tended by dedicated microbial gardeners, ensuring a bountiful fungal harvest.

To ensure teamwork, much like leaf-cutter ants, termites use clear communication. Termites engage in a unique "fungus dance," transferring spores throughout the colony and ensuring fair distribution of this vital resource. This synchronized swaying not only spreads the fungal bounty, but serves to coordinate colony activities and maintain social cohesion. So, there you have it—the whimsical blueprint of the termite.

Exploring the evolutionary journey of termite funiculture unveils the captivating co-evolution interplay between termites and fungi. This captivating natural spectacle hasn't escaped the notice of keen observers. By comparing this distinctive behavior with similar practices among other fungus-farming insects—like the attine ants and ambrosia beetles—we uncover intriguing parallels and distinct adaptations within each group.

The emergence of termite funiculture from a singular ancestral line stands as a testament to nature's ingenuity. It reminds us that the most astonishing tales of mutualism and adaptation often lie hidden in the most unexpected corners of the natural world.

Now let's explore the intricacies, benefits, and evolutionary significance of this mutualistic behavior. Certain termite species, such as fungus-growing termites of the Macrotermitidae family, engage in an obligate mutualism with fungi of the genus *Termitomyces*. These termites cultivate the fungi in specialized chambers known as fungus gardens within their nests.

To establish these gardens, termites feed pre-chewed plant material—indigestible for themselves—to the fungi. They await the fungi's conversion of this material into a digestible food source, fostering the growth of substantial mushrooms. The termites then consume both the mushrooms and the transformed plant material, a nutritious meal beneficial for the queen and larvae. This rich food source, produced through cellulose and lignin breakdown in plant cell walls by the fungi, yields a protein-rich fungal mycelium. This sustenance leads to prolific egg production by the well-nourished queen. The termites offer protection while the fungi provide nourishment, fostering a harmonious coexistence.

Above ground, the termites construct their mounds using saliva, feces, and clay—known locally as muruduns. Deep within the labyrinthine tunnels lie intricate chambers housing the fungus gardens, the engine rooms of this symbiotic relationship. These gardens provide a controlled environment with optimal temperature and humidity for fungal growth.

Worker termites fashion a paste from undigested wood, using it to maintain the chambers, inoculating it with fungal spores. These tireless architects toil in darkness, tending to their delicate gardens with unwavering dedication. They regulate growth conditions to suit the demanding *Termitomyces* cultures. The fungi, alchemists of cellulose and lignin, transform indigestible plant material into a feast of nutrients for the termites.

As the fungus gardens peak, *Termitomyces titanicus* reveals its majestic fruiting bodies. Its reddish-brown caps, adorned with the wrinkles of time, burst forth, releasing a shower of spores beyond the termite mound. This colossal edible mushroom boasts shield-sized caps—one of the world's largest mushroom species. This incredible fungus grows from the center of termite mounds, showcasing nature's artistic prowess with cap diameters of up to 3 feet and heights exceeding 2 feet. Pinkish spores and an elongated stipe called a pseudorhiza, linking them to the comb within the termite nest, distinguish these fungi. Many species also showcase a pronounced umbo, or papilla, known as a perforatorium, aiding their remarkable skill to penetrate surrounding soil—their perseverance evident in their capacity to push through. The perforatorium is the part of the sperm that penetrates the egg, so you can see the tenacity to push.

Termite fungiculture serves as a striking example of mutualism in nature. The cultivation of fungi provides termites with a dependable food source, while termites offer an ideal growth environment for the fungi. By scrutinizing termite fungiculture, we unravel the intricate web of interactions and glean insights into cooperative farming.

Through a dance of mutualism, fungal strains frequently exchange between termite lineages within each farming group, much like farmers experimenting with different crops to optimize yields. Termites have become agriculturalists in the fungal realm, nurturing a relationship far beyond the ordinary.

Ambrosia Beetles: Fungal Farmland Architects

Ambrosia beetles have also proven to be expert fungi farmers. Like termites, ambrosia beetles eat wood and need fungi to break down the wood into a more usable form. These *Xyleborus spp.*, belonging to the vast weevil family Curculionidae, rank among the myriad species in this expansive animal clan, comprising diverse weevils and bark beetles, including the illustrious ambrosia beetles. Considered pests for their penchant for tunneling into wood, these beetles are notorious for propagating tree diseases and inflicting damage. Thriving worldwide, they inhabit various environments, from forests to urban landscapes. Their modus operandi involves burrowing into trees, introducing fungal spores that foster a symbiotic alliance with the beetles. The beetle's existence depends on eight fungal species in the genus *Raffaelea*. These ambrosia fungi release volatiles that attract the beetles. The beetles support and collect fungi within the tree, consuming it as nourishment, while benefiting the fungi.

In case you are not familiar with the body shape of the ambrosia beetle, allow me to introduce you to the industrious beetle! Its armor-like outer shell, constructed from chitin, gives it the appearance of a tank and ensures unwavering safety against the hazards of the outside world. With a jaw that could rival a chainsaw, this pint-sized lumberjack has earned the title of

"Mandibular Might" for cutting through wood like scissors through paper. Equipped with pincers that function like Swiss Army knives, they are ready for any challenge. Deep within their cozy wood tunnels, these beetles showcase their home-building skills. And let's not forget the antenna antics! With their antennae waving in the air like symphony conductors, these beetles have mastered the art of bug communication.

While their eye structure might seem modest, affording them only the ability to discern light from darkness, it serves as a rudimentary window to the world. Despite their limited vision, their remarkable sense of smell compensates for it, allowing them to navigate through a labyrinth of scents in their quest for food and companionship.

Visualize these industrious beetles as miniature lumberjacks, each equipped with a specialized mycangium, a pouch derived from the Latin mycangium, designed for carrying fungal spores. These pouches, first described by Helen Franke Grossmen in 1956 and later elaborated on by Lekh R. in 1963, serve as a vital reservoir for fungi, sustaining both the beetles and their larvae throughout their life cycle within the tree's galleries. What fascinates me is that different species have unique mycangia or pouches, similar to how we have all different purses, bags, or wallets. The beetle pouches can come in various other shapes, such as coils, spheres, or discs. The presence of such anatomical pouch differences helps classify ambrosia beetles.

Ambrosia beetles and bark beetles might be mistaken for one another, but they have distinct behaviors and ecological roles. Bark beetles tunnel into the bark and feed on the phloem, disrupting the tree's transports of sugars.

These tunnels disrupt the flow of nutrients and water, leaving the tree weakened and vulnerable. Unlike ambrosia beetles, bark beetles do not farm fungi for sustenance. Ethanol, a chemical produced by a weakened or dying tree, attracts both beetle types. Bark beetles often colonize stressed or dying trees, contributing to the decomposition process. Some species of bark beetle attack healthy trees, especially during outbreaks when their populations are high. They may release pheromones that attract other beetles to mass-attack trees, causing extensive damage to forests.

Unlike their bark beetle brethren, ambrosia beetles are more like meticulous farmers. They carve elaborate galleries within the xylem, which is the water transport tissue in the tree's woody core, not for food, but to cultivate their very own fungal farms! These galleries become havens for both the beetles and their precious fungi. Think intricate tunnels packed with fungal hyphae, resembling sawdust—a far cry from the bark beetles' meandering phloem-chasing routes.

Let's move on to the relationship between the ambrosia fungi and ambrosia beetle. The fungi have two primary forms: filamentous and yeast-like. The gallery hosts the growth of filamentous fungi, whereas the mycangium transports the yeast-like form of fungi along with the spores. Female ambrosia beetles bore through the bark to create fungal rich galleries where they lay their eggs. The fungi break down the wood, providing a food source for the beetles and their larvae, which grow in the nutrient rich nursery. The larvae, nestled within the nurturing embrace of the fungal mycelium, thrive on the abundant supply of nutrients that their fungal partners provide. This partnership ensures not only the survival but also the flourishing of the next generation of ambrosia beetles.

The beetles carry fungal spores from their original host tree to new trees when they disperse. While some species of bark beetles may carry fungi on their bodies, helping in dispersal, they do not cultivate fungi as part of their life cycle. The ambrosia beetle is a delightful blend of charm, craftsmanship, and bug charisma—an insect mushroom farmer extraordinaire!

Chapter 5

The Poop Squad
(Coprophilous *Fungi*)

*Life is like a mushroom, it grows in the dark but
finds beauty in the light.*
~Unknown

Coprophilous fungi are the connoisseurs of dung, the epicureans of excrement! These fungi have developed a rather unique taste for the finer things in life—animal feces. Yes, you heard that right—they're fungi with a penchant for poop. Now, it might seem like a crappy job, but someone's got to do it, right? Dung-loving fungi have evolved to exploit the rich nutrients present in animal feces and play a vital role in ecosystems by breaking down the organic matter found in feces, recycling it, and returning essential nutrients to the soil.

These filamentous fungi (coprophiles) carpet surrounding vegetation with their spores. Grazing herbivores unknowingly ingest these spores when eating vegetation. Within the animal's digestive tract, the spores endure a perilous journey—an acidic gauntlet—before emerging unharmed onto the fertile landscape of dung. The very existence of coprophilous fungi hinges on the grazing patterns of herbivores. Cattle, horses, moose, and countless other grazers serve as unwitting partners in this intricate dance of decomposition and nutrient release.

Dung-loving fungi—those tireless recyclers of the poop-world—work a magic trick no human composting bin can mimic. Like alchemists, they devour the complex leftovers of herbivores, pulverizing tough organic molecules into a rich assortment of soil nutrients. This nutrient bonanza acts like a potent fertilizer, pumping up the soil's vitality and turning it into a plant paradise. And guess who gets to feast on this lush new garden? The herbivores and plants engage in a beneficial relationship, creating a delightful cycle of exchange. When a pastured friend leaves a "deposit," remember—it's not just waste, it's an invitation to a feast for fungi, who pay back the favor by turning leftovers into lifeblood for the ecosystem.

Surviving digestion is not an easy feat. One remarkable adaptation of coprophilous fungi is the thick-cell wall of their spores, enabling survival through digestion and germination in the dung with minimal competition from other organisms. This armored resilience grants them safe passage, eventually depositing them in the land of 'cow' patties. Here, amidst a nutrient cornucopia, fungal filaments weave a mycelial network across the fertile landscape. And then, the grand finale: fruiting bodies rise like miniature towers, launching countless spores on the wind, rain, or animal rides. These dispersal methods carry the fungal legacy, seeking new locations.

Just like humans have their culinary preferences, coprophiles are picky eaters when it comes to their favorite droppings. The elegant *Coprinus radiatus* likes horse patties, while the dapper *Panaeolus campanulatus* prefers cow patties. Others, like the adventurous *Panaeolus sphinctrinus*, are more versatile, relishing both refined equine and bovine cuisine while still indulging in the occasional rustic moose dung.

Psilocybe spp, known as "magic mushrooms," has a unique association with herbivore dung that is intriguing. These mushrooms are members of the genus *Psilocybe*, which includes several species known for their psychoactive properties, because of the presence of compounds such as psilocybin and psilocin. These mind-bending fungi have cultivated a fascinating relationship with herbivore patties. Not only do they favor herbivore dung, but their very essence, the psychoactive compounds, appears linked to their dietary choice. Psilocybin might be a dung-derived defense mechanism. Some scientists hypothesize that psilocybin and psilocin serve as a clever defense mechanism for *Psilocybe*. These chemicals might deter dung-loving insects from munching on their precious mycelia, ensuring their survival and spore dispersal. It can also act as an attractant for animals, namely humans, looking for a psychedelic experience. This aids in the dispersal of spores.

Specific species have developed intricate mechanisms to catapult their spores across vast distances, guaranteeing their widespread dispersal. Enter *Pilobolus*, hailed as the undefeated leader of the 'poop squadron.' These fungi transcend ordinary spore dissemination; they resemble the ballistic launchers of the fungal realm, equipped with an unparalleled spore-propelling tactic. Mycologists dub them 'hat throwers' or the 'shotgun fungus.' In an earlier chapter, I detailed how the lungworm nematode hitch-hikes amidst these explosive launches.

Imagine a tiny, pressure-building balloon. That's *Pilobolus*' secret weapon: a sporangiophore. This special-ized stalk grows tall, culminates in a pouch called a spo-rangium, and packs it full of spores. Inside, fluid builds up, creating incredible turgor pressure. Then, boom! The sporangium tip explodes, transforming into a microscopic cannon. But here's the twist: these aren't mere dud mis-siles. Launched by the bursting pressure, *Pilobolus*'s spores shoot through the air at impressive speeds, traveling mul-tiple meters away from the fecal launch pad. *Pilobolus* is the Olympic gold medalist of spore dispersal. This disper-sal mechanism allows *Pilobolus* to colonize new territories with remarkable efficiency.

But its story doesn't end there. *Pilobolus* has a fas-cinating symbiotic relationship with grazing animals. Herbivores and their dung are crucial for *Pilobolus*'s life cycle. *Pilobolus* thrives in herbivore dung, breaking it down and speeding up the decomposition process. Think of them as tiny recycling plants, breaking down waste and releasing essential nutrients back into the soil, contribut-ing to the functioning and balance of natural ecosystems. So, the next time you see a grazing animal, remember its hidden role in facilitating the incredible feats of *Pilobolus* and other coprophilous fungi.

The Potential in Studying Coprophilous Fungi Going Beyond Poop

The allure of coprophilous fungi for diverse industries stems from their remarkable capability to generate enzymes adept at breaking down complex plant cell wall polymers. These polymers include cellulose, hemicelluloses, and lignin. These marvels are within reach, thanks to the dung-loving fungi and their potent "secretomes," the cocktails of enzymes they produce. This "green gold" holds immense potential for industries seeking sustainable solutions. Imagine textiles spun from plant fibers broken down by fungal enzymes, detergents empowered by nature's cleaning agents, or biofuels fueled by cellulose transformed into liquid energy. Beyond industrial use, these fungi boast medicinal qualities and have found integration within pharmaceuticals.

In the wildlife dung of Kenya, biologists have delved into coprophilous fungi, extracting species from the African elephant, Cape buffalo, dik-dik, giraffe, impala, and waterbuck. Armed with the latest molecular tools, researchers are uncovering a hidden diversity within this fungal family, shedding light on new species and whispering tantalizing possibilities. Understanding these enigmatic Coprophilous fungi is more than just academic curiosity—it's crucial for several reasons. First, they serve as pivotal indicators of habitat diversity. Second, they contribute to the decomposition of organic matter, enhancing soil fertility. Third, select species are edible and offer an alternative source of protein. Fourth, we can use them for medicinal purposes. Finally, their enzyme cocktails hold the key to unlocking a cleaner future in industry. Imagine fields of energy crops yielding biofuels through the magic of fungal enzymes, a sustainable solution to our dependence on fossil fuels. These versatile microorganisms offer a glimpse into a greener tomorrow, where nature's alchemy fuels our world.

Dung Detectives: How Fungi Whisper Secrets of Ancient Mammals

Another intriguing facet of coprophilous fungi lies in their significant role in paleontology. These fungi serve as invaluable tools for examining fossil mammals by scrutinizing the unique signature of spores and other fungal remnants preserved within fossilized animal dung, or coprolites. Through coprolite analysis, researchers glean insights into the dietary patterns, behaviors, and ecological dynamics of ancient mammals. By dissecting these fossilized coprophilous fungi, scientists can reconstruct the plant menus of long-gone mammals. We can identify the grasses and shrubs that sustained these giants. We learn not just who ate what, but what landscapes teemed with life millions of years ago. A time capsule to our past.

The distribution of coprophilous fungi serves as a dependable gauge of herbivorous animal presence and abundance within ecosystems of yesteryears. By pinpointing these fungi in coprolites, researchers reconstruct the past environments inhabited by herbivorous mammals. This knowledge aids in unraveling ancient ecosystems, discerning alterations in vegetation, and comprehending shifts in climate.

Coprophilous fungi also act as indicators of the conditions conducive to dung preservation—factors like humidity, temperature, and substrate types. Understanding these elements contributes to unraveling the coprolite formation processes and subsequent preservation. Because of their abbreviated life cycle, these fungi provide a means to date coprolites. By analyzing the periodic release of their spores, researchers can estimate the season or even year herbivores deposited the dung. This technique allows us to correlate coprolites with other fossil evidence, building a robust timeline of prehistoric events.

In summary, coprophilous fungi act as Rosetta stones for interpreting the language of coprolites. They unveil the diets, behaviors, and environments of vanished mammals, painting a vivid picture of prehistoric ecosystems. From unraveling ancient food webs to reconstructing long-lost landscapes, these dung-loving fungi illuminate the natural history of mammals and the forgotten worlds they once roamed.

So, the next time you smell a whiff of farm fresh dung, remember the silent storytellers hidden within. These coprophilous fungi, whispering secrets from the past, are a testament to the hidden wonders unearthed by curiosity and scientific ingenuity. They're not just fascinating; they're essential players in piecing together the puzzle of life on Earth, one fossilized dropping at a time.

Chapter 6

Pollinators and Fungi: Unveiling Their Interwoven Relationship

*If the bee disappeared off the surface of the globe,
then man would have only four years of life left.
"No more bees, no more pollination, no more
plants, no more animals, no more man.*

~ Unknown

The link between fungi and the world of pollinating creatures, from bees to bats, is an intricate tale of mutual influence often overlooked. While pollinators rarely dine on mushrooms, their health and survival depends on these fungal wonders.

Forget mere snacks—mushrooms emerge as unsung heroes, offering much more than meets the eye. A primary impact lies in the nutrient-packed arsenal they offer, channeling vitamins, minerals, and amino acids crucial for the growth and reproduction of pollinators. Mycorrhizal fungi form symbiotic bonds with host plants, bolstering their constitution and indirectly benefiting the pollinating pals.

But it doesn't end there. Fungi coordinate a harmonious interplay of attraction and protection, emitting volatile compounds to entice pollinators while producing defensive substances to repel threats posed by predators and parasites that pose a danger to our valuable pollinators. Their influence extends to providing safe havens—dense clusters of mushrooms fashion protective microclimates, a sanctuary shielding pollinators from harsh environmental onslaughts.

Yet, their contribution transcends mere shelter. The very remains of these fungal marvels, their decomposing bodies, become the fertile cradle for new life. Think of a fallen log adorned with oyster mushrooms—not just a decaying relic, but a nursery for future wildflowers. These new blooms paint the landscape with vibrant colors, beckoning more pollinators into the fungal realm, perpetuating the cycle of life and pollination.

This intricate relationship between fungi and pollinators remains veiled in mystery, urging for deeper exploration. Yet, one thing is clear—mushrooms are not silent bystanders in the process of pollination. Fungi are crucial players, aiding in the health and prosperity for the creatures that keep our gardens buzzing and our plates full.

Protecting these essential agents of nature is a matter of urgency. Creating and preserving habitats, curtailing the use of harmful pesticides, and embracing sustainable agricultural practices that nurture fungal diversity are not just ecological imperatives—they're acts of gratitude for the silent heroes who fuel the buzz of life around us. Recognizing the irreplaceable role of pollinators and their fungal allies within our food systems and ecosystems is the linchpin for a sustainable future, where human harmony with the natural world flourishes, just like the vibrant mushrooms dotting our landscapes.

Bees and Fungi: A Flourishing Connection for Our Food and Future

The relationship between bees and fungi blends the disciplines of entomology, mycology, and ecology to unravel the interconnectedness of these organisms. The Western honeybee, *Apis mellifera*, contributes significantly to crop pollination and global food production. Because the honeybee is so crucial to our ecosystem, its decline from colony collapse syndrome has fueled extensive research, with experts like Paul Stamets leading the charge.

Stamets, a renowned mycologist and advocate for fungal applications in medicine and the environment, has spotlighted mushrooms' pivotal role in bolstering bee health. Stamets' work with the horse's hoof fungus, *Fomes fomentarius*, illustrates this approach. He observed bees naturally drawn to this fungus, hypothesizing it offered medicinal benefits. His research, detailed in his 2018 study, confirmed this. Extracts of *Fomes fomentarius* exhibited antiviral properties against viruses like deformed wing virus (DWV), a major contributor to colony collapse disorder. By providing bees with these extracts, Stamets aimed to boost their immune system and fight off viral infections.

The threats bees face extend beyond viruses. Pesticides weaken their immune systems, leaving them vulnerable to disease. Interestingly, Stamets found the mycelium of certain fungi, including Fomes fomentarius, possesses the remarkable ability to break down various environmental toxins. This makes them potential allies in detoxifying bees and mitigating the harmful effects of pesticides.

Varroa destructor mites stand as another threat to bee populations worldwide, perpetuating colony collapse. Enter fungi, *Metarhizium anisopliae*, which has emerged as a natural contender to combat *Varroa* mite infestations. This fungus specializes in infiltrating and consuming various insect pests, including *Varroa* mites. It adheres to the mites' bodies, penetrating their exoskeletons and eventually killing them. Studies have demonstrated its efficacy in curbing mite infestations and fostering bee colony health.

Researcher Dr. Sara Klee delves into the secrets of fungi, searching for weapons against honeybee diseases, while Dr. Lori Carris investigates the complex dance between bees and fungi in forest ecosystems. Their work at the USDA Agricultural Research Service and Oregon State University highlights the many angles of this critical issue.

As we face the decline of bee populations, crucial for food production and ecosystem health, we must understand and foster these bee-fungus partnerships. The research in this area is still young, but the potential benefits are vast. From boosting bee immunity to combat pests and detoxifying environments, fungi offer a promising array of tools in our fight to protect these crucial pollinators. By nurturing this connection, we can ensure a flourishing future for bees, for ourselves, and for the ecosystems that sustain us.

Butterflies, Moths, and
the Hidden Relationship with Fungi

Nature's intricate web often binds the unlikeliest of creatures in surprising partnerships. While bee-mushroom bonds have buzzed with research, the fascinating interplay between butterflies, moths, and fungi has fluttered under the radar. But recent discoveries are peeling back the petals on these captivating connections, revealing tales of pollination, gourmet feasts, and growth spurts that would make any caterpillar do a jig. Here are a few studies, offering insights into butterfly and moth interactions with fungi.

In the lush rainforests of Costa Rica, researchers stumbled upon a secret society of mushroom mycophiles. Researchers observed *Electrostrymon denarius*, a mysterious butterfly caterpillar, feasting on a fungus. This groundbreaking discovery by Nishida and Robbins (2020) not only unveiled the caterpillar's hidden diet but also blew the doors open on the culinary versatility of caterpillars. Turns out, these caterpillars can savor a wider range of food than we ever imagined, including the earthy delights of fungi. This discovery not only expands our knowledge of caterpillar cuisine but also highlights the interdependence between butterflies and mushrooms.

In Europe, another study by Franziska Eberl (2023) unraveled the picky palates of gypsy moths (*Lymantria dispar*). It turns out the moths have a serious sweet tooth for the rust fungi (*Melamspora*) that produce mannitol, a sugary treat that sends their taste buds into overdrive. However, there's more to it than just sweetness. The real prize lies in the hidden treasure trove of Vitamin B. When offered an assortment of fungal spore-infected and black poplar leaves, the moth larvae became selective foodies, zeroing in on the fungus-laden options. Eberl revealed that caterpillars feasting on fungi grew faster and pupated earlier, giving them a leg up (or rather, a wing up) over their leaf-munching siblings. Turns out, the infected leaves were bursting with essential nutrients like amino acids, nitrogen, and B vitamins.

These studies are more than just juicy gossip about the insect world—they paint a vivid picture of the intricate relationships that bind butterflies, moths, and fungi. *Electrostrymon denarius* caterpillar's mushroom munching expands our understanding of caterpillar diets, hinting at their potential role in spreading fungal spores. And who knew gypsy moths were such keen mycophagists, using their sophisticated senses to identify and exploit the nutritional goldmine within fungus-infected leaves?

Monarchs and Milkweed-Fungi Symbiotic Shield

But the fungal fun doesn't stop there. Take the majestic monarch butterfly (*Danaus plexippus*), facing challenges that could clip their wings forever. Habitat loss and a grueling multi-generational migration threaten their very existence. During their epic journey, they rely on specific plants for fuel and baby-rearing grounds. Enter milkweed (*Asclepias spp.*), the Monarch's secret weapon and sole source of sustenance for their caterpillars. But milkweed's benefit goes beyond a tasty leaf; it produces cardenolides, a steroid toxin that acts like a chemical shield for the

Monarch caterpillars. This toxin, potent enough to send other animals' hearts racing, deters predators like birds and insects, and keeps parasites at bay. As the caterpillars munch away, they hoard these cardenolides like a stash of forbidden treats, carrying them over into their butterfly stage. It's like an insect version of a chemical arsenal, ready to repel any unsuspecting predator with a toxic payload.

The Monarch's vibrant colors and unpleasant taste work hand-in-hand with cardenolides to create a predator-proof package, a phenomenon known as prey avoidance. But here's the twist: the health of milkweed and its cardenolide production depend on the mutualistic partnership with plant root fungi called arbuscular fungi. These fungi form a symbiotic relationship with the milkweed, boosting its cardenolide production and benefiting both partners. And guess what? Monarchs raised on milkweed with higher cardenolide levels are healthier, with fewer infections, parasites, and diseases. By protecting milkweed and its fungal partners, we can help shield the Monarchs and preserve their awe-inspiring beauty and ecological importance.

Hummingbirds: Nature's Tiny Fungal Delivery Service

Hummingbirds, those dazzling feathered jewels of the garden, are renowned for their acrobatic displays and insatiable appetite for nectar. But their ecological roles extend far beyond sipping floral sweets. Recent research suggests that these miniature marvels play a crucial role in the fascinating world of fungi, acting as unwitting couriers for their microscopic spores.

Imagine a hummingbird flitting from flower to flower, its iridescent feathers dusted with a vibrant mix of pollen. Unbeknownst to the bird, some of these pollen grains harbor tiny fungal passengers—spores waiting for a chance to disperse and colonize new hosts. As the hummingbird dives into another blossom, these spores brush off its body, finding themselves deposited on a fresh canvas, ready to germinate and spread the fungus's reach.

To date, there has been a shortage of research on any potential mutualistic benefits between fungi and hummingbirds. However, researchers Carlos Lara and Juan Francisco Ornelas (2003) have documented a fascinating example of hummingbird-fungal interactions. They studied the partnership between the *Moussonia deppeana* plant and the *Amazilia violiceps* hummingbird. In this mutualistic interplay, a fungus called *Fusarium moniliforme* infects the plant's flowers, prompting them to produce an extra bounty of nectar. This sugary lure attracts the hummingbirds, who, in their nectar-guzzling frenzy, become unwitting couriers for the fungus's spores. The hummingbirds enjoy an abundant feast, while the fungus secures a ride to new flowers, ensuring its propagation.

Unfortunately, this symbiotic relationship isn't always a fairy tale. *Fusarium moniliforme*, while a boon for the *Moussonia* plant in specific circumstances, can also act as a pathogen in other contexts, causing corn rot and even some human diseases. Hummingbirds, in their frequent floral visits, can also pick up spores of various fungal diseases, including anther smut, *Botrytis* blight, powdery mildew, and rust. These tiny avian pollinators play a complex role in the fungal world, acting as both beneficial dispersers and unwitting vectors of disease.

Bats: Nature's Nighttime Spore Squad

Forget the spooky stereotypes! Bats are the dark knights of the ecological world, orchestrating a nocturnal flyby of fungal spore dispersal across diverse ecosystems. These winged mammals, belonging to the Chiroptera order ("hand-wing" in Greek!), use echolocation to devour millions of pesky insects (mosquitoes, beware!). But their talents extend far beyond bug zapping. Fruit-eating bats, especially species of the Phyllostomidae family, are champion pollinators in tropical and subtropical havens. From agave and coffee to corn and beyond, bats that feed on fruits play a crucial role in countless crops.

But their ecological magic doesn't stop there. Bats take on a fascinating second act as fungal spore spreaders, though their methods differ from their hummingbird counterparts. Picture this: bats have a sweet tooth for fruit, often coated with fungal spores. As they indulge, these spores hitch a ride through the bat's digestive system, eventually emerging in their guano (bat poop, to put it plainly). When guano splatters to the ground, it becomes a launch pad for the spores, sending them on their merry way to colonize new plants. Some fungi have even evolved to become BFFs with bats. Take *Penicillium chrysogenum*, the producer of penicillin, regularly found chilling in bat excrement. Talk about a gutsy partnership!

Scientists Chaverri P. and G. Chaverri (2022) have been digging into this secret world, discovering why fruit-eating bats are such stellar fungal disseminators. Their secret weapons? Long-distance flights, in-flight guano bombs, and a digestive system that keeps fungal spores alive and kicking. These aerial acrobats can spread spores across vast distances, even bridging gaps through deforested areas lacking helpful fungi. Unlike their birds, bats have a knack for exploring damaged areas, boosting the health of tropical ecosystems by delivering beneficial fungal spores. With the onset of global fires, the importance of bats as spore dispensers should encourage forthcoming investigations of bat-plant-fungi mutualistic networks. Next time you hear a bat flitting through the night, remember: they're not just spooky shadows or disease vectors. They're spreading life and vitality in the darkness, one spore at a time.

Chapter 7

Connecting the Dots: Exploring the Link Between Herpetology and Mycology

> *This morning when I woke up I felt good because the sun was shining. I felt good because I was a frog. And I felt good because I have you as a friend."*
> ~ARNOLD LOBEL, *Days with Frog and Toad*

Delving into the fascinating world of amphibians and reptiles, herpetologists unravel the mysteries of these captivating cold-blooded vertebrates. Amphibians, ranging from frogs to salamanders, boast incredible diversity, dwelling in water during pivotal stages of their lifecycle. In contrast, reptiles like snakes and lizards adapted to terrestrial life.

But where does the world of fungi intersect with these creatures? Amphibians, as predators, show no interest in eating mushrooms. Reptiles primarily eat insects, mammals, and plants, and on rare occasions consume mushrooms. In fact, some reptiles can be seen frolicking near ponds in search of unexpected delicacy: mushrooms.

As someone who spends a lot of time poking around damp, shady places (prime real estate for both mushrooms and cold-blooded creatures), I've seen my fair share of surprising encounters. A flash of movement near a large bolete mushroom might be a curious salamander, while a coiled copperhead could be curled up beside a patch of honey mushrooms. I've always known they prefer shady habitats, but I didn't realize the herpetology fungal connection until I started researching animal mycophiles.

Despite scarce documentation on reptilian mycophagy, researchers have noted specific tortoise species foraging and feasting on mushrooms in the wild. This revelation throws open a vault of questions. Could vegetarian lizards, masters of plant-based cuisine, hold the key to unlocking an even deeper fungal connection? Why would any creature, let alone a reptile, choose to nibble on fungus? Is it a source of essential nutrients, a medicinal marvel, or a delicious distraction?

Join me on a captivating journey through damp ecosystems and sun-dappled forests as we untangle the threads of this mycological mystery. We'll meet the reptilian mycophiles and discover how the fields of herpetology and mycology intertwine. Prepare to have your preconceptions about nature challenged, your curiosity piqued, and your appetite for knowledge whetted as we embark on this expedition into the tangled realms of reptiles and fungi. First, let's not forget our amphibious friends and their indirect connection to mushrooms, adding another twist to this already intriguing tale.

Toadstools: A Tangled Tale
of Folklore and Fact

The Curious Coexistence of Frogs and Fungi

In the wondrous theater of nature, frogs and fungi share an unexpected kinship, painting a vivid portrait of interwoven existence in ecosystems. While amphibians might seem worlds apart, their connection reveals a captivating narrative, showcasing a fascinating tale of coexistence, one that whispers of delicate ecological balances and the intricate web that binds all living things.

Let's not forget—frogs and toads, renowned insectivores, go where the insects often seek sustenance: mushrooms. Meanwhile, fungi often form mycorrhizal relationships with plants, their delicate threads weaving through the soil, exchanging nutrients. But here's the twist: insects, drawn to mushrooms like moths to a flame, create an insect feast for hungry amphibians. Tongue unfurling like a lightning bolt to snatch insects mid-munch, it's like a frog 24/7 drive-thru right at your doorstep!

But this culinary connection goes beyond a simple meal. The munching and crunching of insects by amphibians might have far-reaching consequences for the plant and mushroom world. Remember those mycorrhizal fungi, the silent partners of plants? By targeting certain insects, frogs could influence the distribution and abundance of these fungal threads, affecting the growth and health of entire plant communities. It's a ripple effect, starting with a frog's flicking tongue and ending with a swaying forest canopy.

Speaking of mushrooms, the word "toadstool" often gets tossed around like a mossy pebble. But unlike a precise scientific term, "toadstool" lacks a defined meaning. Some say it refers to the sturdy base of a mushroom, the "stool" upon which the cap sits. Linguists suggest its German roots, *Todesstuhl*, translate to "death's chair," a grim reminder of the poisonous perils some fungi hold. Based on the literature, I have always associated toadstools with toxic mushrooms. Perhaps the association with toads stems from their shared love of damp, shady nooks. Or maybe it's the whimsical resemblance of certain mushroom caps to a toad's bumpy skin. Whatever the reason, these two creatures have found their way into folklore and fairy tales, often depicted as partners in mystical realms. From witches' brews to enchanted forests, toads and mushrooms have become synonymous with the magical and the marvelous.

Let's venture into the realm of folklore and mythology, where frogs and fungi take center stage as mystical emissaries. Legends paint frogs as conduits, bridging our mortal world with ethereal realms. The bright colors and unique shapes of toadstools (think fly agaric) have led them being connected to enchanted realms and supernatural beings. And the promise of psychedelic shamanic journeys. Woven into the fabric of folklore, they serve as companions to witches, wizards, and magical beings, invoking a sense of wonder and mystique that transcends time. Fast forward to today, and the whimsical charm of this unlikely duo has found a new home in the Cottagecore aesthetic—a trend that romanticizes simple living and natural beauty. This style embraces the cozy allure of cottages, traditional crafts, and a deep connection to nature.

And guess what often finds its way into Cottagecore art and décor? You guessed it—the endearing partnership of frogs or toads and mushrooms.

In this captivating narrative, the myth of the frog and mushroom unveils a profound metaphor for environmental harmony and equilibrium. Yet, although my book focuses on the beneficial relationships between animals and fungi, I would be remiss in not mentioning the silent killer that amphibians are facing: chytrid.

This waterborne fungal villain called *Batrachochytrium dendrobatidis* (Bd), attacks the keratin layer of frogs' skin. Bd weakens their immune systems, disrupts their ability to breathe, and even throws their heart rhythms into disarray. The consequences are devastating. Since its emergence in the 1990s, chytrid has triggered mass die-offs, silencing countless frog choruses around the globe. Imagine the eerie silence where exuberant croaks once filled the air—a stark reminder of this hidden threat.

Beyond its direct impact on amphibians, chytrid disrupts ecosystems, affecting mosquito populations and altering pest control dynamics. Amphibians are also crucial biological indicators of environmental health, reflecting the well-being of both aquatic and terrestrial ecosystems. They're like detectives, uncovering hidden imbalances caused by pollution and environmental changes. Our 'canary in the coalmine.'

These remarkable creatures play a pivotal role in medical research, offering insights into limb regeneration and producing compounds with pharmaceutical potential.

So, where does chytrid find its foothold? The trade of wildlife, like a Trojan horse, transports Bd across borders. By curbing wildlife trade and implementing stricter biosecurity protocols, we can weaken the chytrid's grip. Let's join the chorus, not of frogs, but of action. By protecting amphibian habitats, minimizing human impact and addressing broader environmental challenges, we can ensure the survival of these captivating creatures and safeguard life on our planet. Let's ensure the chytrid's shadow doesn't silence the croaks of tomorrow. In my ideal world, a regal frog would sit atop a mushroom throne, feasting on insects and igniting the creative fires of any artist lucky enough to observe this spectacle.

Beyond Prey and Plants: The Unexpected Feast of Fungi in the Reptile World

Forget crickets and lettuce. Some reptiles developed a taste for gourmet fungi! Delving into their surprising dining habits unlocks a hidden world, where creatures we thought we knew are defying labels with a penchant for mushrooms. This isn't just the occasional nibble, mind you. A study, "Reptilian Mycophagy: A global review of mutually beneficial associations" by Elliott, Bower, and Vernes, dives deep into this fascinating relationship, revealing a complex web of benefits for both reptile and fungus. Prepare to be surprised by the unexpected twists and turns in the world of reptilian cuisine!

Recent revelations, drawing from observations of diverse reptilian species, have unveiled the captivating trend of reptiles adding fungi to their menu. Cooper and Vermes' investigation spotlighted larger-bodied skinks, such as those hailing from the genera *Tiliqua* and *Egernia*, revealing mycophagy. Take the Eastern Blue-tongued

Lizard, a larger-bodied skink belonging to the Tiliqua genus. Imagine witnessing this lizard, excavating beneath a Coastal Rosemary shrub, its powerful claws unearthing a hidden treasure—a white, ball-shaped fungal mass reminiscent of an immature stinkhorn or anemone fungi. But this wasn't just any buried object; with gusto, the lizard savored this unexpected snack. Not convinced? When presented with the recovered fungus, it devoured it, solidifying the evidence of reptilian mycophagy and igniting a wave of curiosity about its ecological significance.

This captivating case isn't an isolated incident. Cooper and Vermes' investigation extends beyond the blue-tongued lizard, spotlighting mycophagy in other *Tiliqua* and *Egernia* skinks—larger-bodied skinks known for their diverse diets. These findings open doors to a hidden world, one where reptiles challenge our preconceived notions and embrace the diverse bounty of the natural world.

But why would a reptile, equipped for munching on greens, turn to fungi? The answer, like many things in nature, is complex and multifaceted. Fungi offer a unique nutritional package, rich in fiber, vitamins, and even essential amino acids that might be missing from a reptile's usual diet.

Beyond the mere novelty of reptiles engaging in mushroom meals, there's a ripple effect on ecosystems. Take the Eastern box turtle (*Terrapene carolina carolina*). A study by S.C. Jones and colleagues revealed these shelled wonders as potential fungal superheroes. Imagine them lumbering through forests, their shells adorned with a mosaic of invisible passengers—fungal spores! By analyzing their fecal samples, the researchers found a treasure trove of spores, representing diverse groups like Ascomycota and Basidiomycota. They even identified specific hitchhikers like the pathogens *Cryptococcus albidus* and *Rhodotorula mucilaginosa*. Considering these turtles' frequent ponds and lakes, the potential for spreading fungal diversity and disease becomes staggering. Could these slowpokes be key players in shaping fungal ecosystems?

A side note about snakes hiding amongst mushrooms on the forest floor: I can't think of a better place for a snake to exploit the natural attraction of rodents to fungi, turning the very bounty of the forest into a deadly lure.

Mushrooms on the reptilian menu? Who would have thought! While reptilian mycophagy might seem like an outlier behavior, the depth of its ecological implications demands further investigation. These revelations not only reshape our understanding of reptile diets and foraging behaviors, but also shed light on their hidden connection with fungi, uncovering a web of life far more intricate than we ever imagined.

Chapter 8

A Glimpse into the World of Bird-Fungi Relationships

Tame birds sing of freedom. Wild birds fly.

~JOHN LENNON

Birds: nature's warm-blooded feathered marvels soar through the sky with a grace that defies gravity. But their wonder goes far beyond their ability to fly. From the dazzling plumage of a peacock to the mesmerizing songs of a nightingale, birds boast a kaleidoscope of adaptations. Their lightweight hollow bones allow for effortless flight, while powerful wings propel them across vast distances. Keen eyesight, often surpassing our own, helps them spot prey from afar, while specialized beaks crack nuts, tear flesh, and sip nectar. Their intricate social behaviors, from elaborate courtship rituals to cooperative hunting, showcase remarkable intelligence and adaptability. Birds are living testaments to evolution's ingenuity, each species a unique masterpiece, forever captivating our hearts and imaginations.

Speaking of birds, have you ever stopped to wonder how those mushroom spores travel such vast distances? Turns out, birds play a starring role in this fascinating game of fungal hide-and-seek! This little-known partnership between birds and fungi, called ornithomycology, is a prime example of nature's intricate web of connections.

Birds inhabit diverse environments and niches, so it's unsurprising they widely disperse fungal spores. Jays gobbling down mushrooms, woodpeckers drilling holes that become fungal havens, flycatchers sporting spores on their feathery coats—these feathered friends are nature's ultimate dispersal agents. Meanwhile, thrashers, ground foraging birds, pick up fungal spores as they transverse through soil and litter. Pigeons and doves, urban nomads of the skies, carry fungal passengers, dispersing them as they navigate cityscapes. Sometimes pigeons can spread fungal-borne disease. Even ducks and waterfowl become wetland spore ferries, spreading fungal diversity across aquatic landscapes.

But it's not just these ambassadors of flight—songbirds, the troubadours of nature, flit through foliage, playing a pivotal role in fungal spore dispersal. And let's not forget raptors or birds of prey, like eagles and hawks, may pick up fungal spores on their talons and feathers as they catch and consume prey. But this partnership isn't just a one-way street. While fungi spread their spores to far-flung corners of the world, birds get a nutritious meal or cozy nesting material. This is a beneficial outcome for both parties.

Elliott and his colleagues' 2019 study, "A Global Review of Avian-Fungal Symbiosis," paints a vivid canvas of these interactions, revealing an awe-inspiring saga. Key findings from the study include bird mycophagy, nesting associations, tree-cavity excavation, bird zoo-chory, thoughts on co-evolution and nesting behavior and health. In scientific corridors, this study uncovers a realm that has long been overshadowed—the realm of ornithomycology. The study found at least 54 bird species indulge in mycophagy, relishing fungi as a significant dietary component. Beyond food, fungi play a surprising role in bird homes. Observations show that thirty-seven bird families use fungi for nest-building. The fungi add strength to the nests and also help to deter parasites with their chemical compounds. Imagine a nest woven with living, growing threads—that's the magic of fungal partnerships.

Beyond the Visible: The Secret Language of Light in Nature

Could it be that the colors and shapes of fungi adapted to the tune of bird feeding behaviors, painting a unique canvas visible to our feathered friends?

Soaring through the twilight sky, a hawk tracks its prey, its keen vision picking up on faint trails invisible to the human eye. This remarkable ability stems from a special gift: birds possess an extra cone cell that allows them to see ultraviolet (UV) light. This invisible spectrum plays a vital role in their lives, aiding them in finding prey and seeds, and even choosing mates. But the story doesn't end there. The world of UV light holds a surprising connection to another fascinating phenomenon: the eerie glow of some mushrooms. The Eastern Jack-O-Lantern Mushroom (*Omphalotus illudens*) is an example of one of 113 currently known to be bioluminescent.

Have you ever stumbled upon a mushroom bathed in an otherworldly glow during a night walk? This captivating spectacle isn't magic, but a product of clever chemistry called bioluminescence. Unlike fireflies, mushrooms don't "glow" in the dark. Instead, they emit a faint light through a fascinating process involving two key players: luciferin and luciferase. Just to note, fungal luciferin. Imagine luciferin as a miniature flashlight bulb, and luciferase as the switch. When oxygen is present, an exciting reaction happens. Luciferase activates luciferin, which then emits a burst of light energy. After the energy diminishes, the "light bulb" goes back to its usual state and is prepared to shine once more.

But why would a mushroom go through all this trouble to create a faint glow? Scientists are still piecing together the puzzle, but some intriguing possibilities emerge. One function can be the removal of by-products of cellular processes. Another hypothesis suggests that these minia-ture spotlights might be a way to attract helpful insects. Just like fireflies use their light to find mates, mushrooms might lure insects to spread their spores far and wide. The light could also act as a warning sign to nighttime nibblers, deterring them from taking a bite. Perhaps the mushrooms are even having secret conversations with each other, using their bioluminescent whispers to com-municate across the forest floor.

While not all mushrooms possess this glowing abil-ity, it's a remarkable example of how nature uses chemis-try to create captivating adaptations. Here's where things get even more interesting: remember those extra cone cells in birds that see UV light? Well, many mushrooms glow under UV light, making them invisible beacons to the special vision of birds. This could be another way for mushrooms to attract insects, but it also raises fascinating questions about potential co-evolution between birds and fungi. Could birds be using this UV glow to find fungal feasts or mushroom loving insects? This highlights the possibility of hidden partnerships and changes in nature. So, the next time you encounter a mushroom bathed in an otherworldly glow, remember the tiny light show happening within, a testament to the hidden wonders of the natural world. And keep in mind the unseen world of ultraviolet light, where birds might play a yet-to-be-discovered role in the fascinating dance between fungi and the forest ecosystem. Further research is necessary to unravel the complexities of this situation.

Where Birds Feast on Fungi and Forest Secrets Bloom

Studies like Alice Lemos Costa's exploration of Shiny Cowbirds (*Molothrus bonariensis*) in Brazil highlight the importance of investigating specific bird-fungal interactions within unique ecosystems. These ground-dwelling birds feasted on sizable mushrooms, their droppings revealing a treasure trove of fungal spores, emphasizing the need to delve deeper into these fascinating relationships. Alice Lemos Costa and her team explored the relationship between Shiny Cowbirds and the edible *Macrolepiota bonaerensis* mushrooms. According to the study, Shiny Cowbirds consume more mushrooms in areas where they are more abundant. These ground-dwelling birds' scat revealed a treasure trove of fungal spores. This study

97

emphasizes the significance of examining and recording distinct avian-fungal interactions within unique ecological contexts, such as the Pampa biome in Brazil. I will explore a few examples of such established mutualistic relations between birds and fungi.

Two unassuming bird species live deep within the Patagonian forests:, the chucao tapaculos, *Scelorichilus rubecula*, and black-throated huet-huets, *Pteroptochos tarnii*. Once thought to be peckish for insects and seeds, these birds have been unmasked as connoisseurs of mycorrhizal fungi, particularly the elusive truffles. Caiafa et al.'s 2021 study, "Discovering the role of Patagonian birds in the dispersal of truffles and other mycorrhizal fungi," illuminates this fascinating relationship between birds and fungi. These feathered truffle hunters play a crucial role in maintaining healthy forest ecosystems by distributing these vital fungal partners.

Truffles, unlike the more flamboyant mushroom, are clandestine treasures of the fungal realm and thrive underground in a mycorrhizal alliance with specific tree species. They exchange nutrients and water with trees like the Nothofagaceae family. But here's the twist: while most mushrooms fling their spores into the air, truffles play a game of intrigue. They've adapted, relying on creatures to consume them and spread their spores.

That's where our avian heroes come in. Unlike the burrowing mammals we assumed to be the top truffle spore dispersers, the chucao tapaculos and black-throated huet-huets have a taste for these earthy delicacies. As they flit through the forest floor, their sharp beaks peck at the telltale mounds that betray the truffles' presence. They gobble them down with gusto, becoming distributors of truffle spores through their droppings.

ANIMAL MYCOPHILES

But this revelation is not new. Indigenous cultures in places like Kuwait and Central Australia have long recognized this avian-fungi bond, using bird behavior and calls to hunt down these hidden fungal gems. Todd Elliott, a grad student at the University of New England, has compiled a list of 18 bird species worldwide that forage for truffles. This list spans continents, highlighting the global nature of the avian-fungi association. This discovery is a breakthrough in our understanding of forest ecosystems. By scattering truffle spores, these birds fortify mycorrhizal networks, vital for nutrient cycling and the health of Patagonian forests.

Research calls for exploration to uncover the bird-fungal ties that sustain biodiversity. But this partnership comes with a flip side. Birds can also spread invasive species and fungal diseases such as *Histoplasmosis* and *Cryptococcosis* across borders and continents. Just like pollen riding the wind, spores hitched on bird feathers can travel vast distances, potentially introducing new threats to faraway ecosystems.

Woodpeckers, Fungi, and Wood: A Natural Trifecta

Cavity-excavating birds, such as woodpeckers, have well-documented associations with decay fungi. Woodpeckers belong to the subfamily Picinae, making them the true maestros of pecking. Their chiseling expertise is legendary, whether it's foraging for sustenance or crafting elaborate nest cavities. Their beaks are precision tools, capable of carving intricate designs into the wood. They have a hard skull made of spongy bone to protect against brain damage from the repeated blows onto the wood. In the grand family tree of birds, woodpeckers are the true pecking masters. They construct intricate nest cavities within deadwood, showcasing their engineering prowess. They've got blueprints in their heads and carpenter's tools in their beaks, creating homes that would make even Frank Lloyd Wright proud.

Imagine yourself as an entomologist, peering into the world of insects hidden within tree crevices. You're armed with your tools, but the woodpecker? It boasts a long tongue armed with barbs and sticky saliva, nature's Velcro for snatching insects from the deepest recesses of tree bark. With bodies adapted for clinging to tree trunks, they possess a daredevil-like ability to defy gravity. Using tail feathers as balancing poles and back toes as anchors, they effortlessly maneuver tree trunks, inspiring envy in tightrope walkers.

Let's explore the fascinating connection between woodpeckers and fungi. Two interesting studies about the White-Headed Woodpecker, *Picoides albolarvatus*, and the Red-cockaded Woodpeckers showcase an interesting relationship with decay polypore fungi.

In the dry coniferous forests of the northwest, the White-headed Woodpecker is a rare and enchanting species. These birds have adapted unique foraging techniques; including probing in bark crevices, surface gleaning, and excavating below the bark. However, their culinary preferences extend beyond the traditional woodpecker diet, as revealed in the study by Watson and Shaw. The researchers observed White-headed Woodpeckers feeding on insects around the Veiled Polypore, *Cryptoporus volvatus*, a widespread decay fungus that colonizes the sapwood of newly dead trees. The polypore is a magnet for bark beetles, hums with insect activity, and as a pupae station, transforming decaying wood into a bustling buffet that beckons the woodpeckers.

This observation raises intriguing questions about the relationship between White-headed Woodpeckers and the veiled polypore. Are these woodpeckers acting as dispersal agents for the fungus? Could the presence of this decay fungus influence the woodpeckers' habitat selection? The study by Watson and Shaw opens a window into the dynamic and interconnected world of forest life, where every organism plays a unique role.

The Red-cockaded Woodpecker takes the spotlight in a study by Jusino et al. titled "Experimental evidence of a symbiosis between Red-cockaded woodpeckers and fungi". Known as ecosystem engineers, these birds carve cavities in live trees, fostering homes for a multitude of species. Samples reveal the woodpeckers carry fungal communities akin to those found in their excavations, hinting at their role in softening wood and aiding fungal colonization.

To further investigate this partnership, researchers conducted a 26-month field experiment by drilling holes in live trees. Half of these excavations were accessible to Red-cockaded Woodpeckers, while the other half were not. The results were astonishing—the excavations accessible to the woodpeckers contained fungal communities resembling those in natural excavations, while the inaccessible ones had different fungal communities. This experiment provided tangible evidence of woodpeckers altering fungal colonization and community composition.

The symbiotic relationships between woodpeckers and fungi are far more complex and vital to ecosystems than imagined. These woodpeckers aren't just excavators; they're facilitators of fungal dispersal, contributing significantly to forest biodiversity. By feeding on insects, woodpeckers keep tree populations healthy, targeting weakened trees and removing harmful infestations. Their abandoned cavities become crucial havens for a diverse array of wildlife, from other birds to mammals and insects. Furthermore, their work accelerates the decay of dead trees, returning essential nutrients to the soil and fueling the forest's life cycle. Understanding these relationships carries profound implications for forest ecology, wildlife management, and conservation efforts.

The Ingenious World of Bowerbirds: How Fungi and Fantastical Architecture Shape Avian Romance

In the enchanting realm of bird courtship, where flamboyant displays and intricate rituals reign supreme, one avian family stands out as the architects of love: the bowerbirds. These avian artisans create elaborate structures, known as bowers, adorned with an eclectic array of objects to captivate potential mates.

Bowerbirds, belong to the Ptilonorhynchidae family with around 20 dazzling species, are native to Australia, New Guinea, and nearby islands. This family features 17 bowerbirds, known for their elaborate courtship rituals that involve constructing elaborate structures and engaging in intricate dances.

Imagine: amidst lush foliage, researchers stumble upon a curious scene. Upturned mushrooms with telltale beak marks lie scattered beside a vibrant blue object, all beneath a tree. This scene reveals the meticulous effort of a young male bowerbird crafting his bachelor pad, selecting even the humblest of organisms—fungi—to woo a mate.

Bowerbirds, with their penchant for vibrant blue hues, weave fungi like the *Lepista nuda*, with its delicate violet-lilac hues, into their elaborate bowers. These fungi not only enhance the visual allure of the bower but the bowerbirds also aid in the dispersal of the spores, forming a fascinating link between animal behavior and ecological processes. This connection between bowerbirds and fungi unveils a hidden facet of animal-fungal interactions, showcasing how symbiotic relationships intertwine with the whims of avian romance.

However, amidst this spectacle, bowerbirds face challenges. Habitat loss, predation, and human disturbances threaten their existence, highlighting the importance of conservation efforts. Legislation, research, and public awareness are crucial in preserving their habitats and ensuring their continued survival.

In the colorful world of bowerbirds, where romance blossoms amidst fungal treasures and architectural marvels, each intricacy serves as a testament to the boundless creativity of nature. As researchers delve deeper into the mysteries of animal-fungal interactions, they unveil a tapestry of connections that shape the ecological landscape. So, the next time you encounter a bowerbird's enchanting display, remember the fungi that adorn its bower—for in the whimsical dance of courtship, even the humblest of critters plays a vital role.

Of Feathers and Fungi

As we delve deeper into the world of ornithomycology, the story continues to unfold. Birds play a crucial role in fungal ecosystems, dispersing spores, shaping habitats, influencing fungal diversity, and using fungi as a food and nesting materials. The complex relationships between birds and fungi highlight how they benefit the ecosystem from insects to trees.

Birds, especially those traversing vast distances, could play a critical role in dispersing fungi in fragmented landscapes. As habitats shrink, spore dispersal may depend more and more on birds as primary agents of spore dispersal, reshaping ecosystems in their flight paths. Birds use fungi and lichen for nesting material, and if they feed on insects, I can't think of a better place to find flying snacks and wormy meals. By understanding these intricate relationships, we gain valuable insights into forest ecology, wildlife management, and conservation efforts. This knowledge reminds us of our responsibility as stewards of this planet, urging us to protect the delicate balance of these fascinating partnerships.

Chapter 9

Mammalian Mycophagy

Furry Fungal Feeders

Consider mammals—they are warm-blooded, have fur or hair, give birth to live offspring, and nurture their young with milk. Mammals experience emotions like us—happiness, sadness, and fear. They form bonds, care for their offspring, and showcase a spectrum of behaviors, from playful antics to cooperation and aggression. They are kindred spirits.

Diversity reigns supreme among mammals, numbering over 5,400 species that span the gamut from the minuscule shrew to the colossal blue whale. They call a wide array of habitats home, from the icy domains of the Arctic to the lush, steamy rainforests, and their significance in these ecosystems is profound. Think seed dispersal, pollination, and population control—mammals play a vital role in all environments.

While spotting a mammal feasting on a mushroom might be easier than glimpsing a worm feeding on a fungus, don't be fooled by their apparent boldness. The nature of most mammals is such that they startle easily and some exhibit a preference for nocturnal activity, particularly for feeding. Despite their elusive nature, we have documentation of mammals indulging in fungus feasts. From nibbling squirrels to truffle-hunting marsupials and even the occasional adventurous primate, mycophagous mammals come in all shapes and sizes. Mammals aid in the dispersal of spores by consuming fungi and excreting them in their feces. Some fungi spores even hitch a ride on mammalian fur or feet. A classic case of zoochory. They spread fungal spores across vast areas. An Australian investigation discovered that bush rats can spread truffle spores up to 100 meters away from the main fungus.

Among the most remarkable spore dispersers is the tapir, the largest land mammal in Central and South America. Because they've changed so little since the Eocene, tapirs are often called living fossils. Although tapirs may resemble a bizarre mix of hippopotamus, pig, and elephant, they're actually closely related to horses and rhinoceroses. Their streamlined bodies and prehensile noses are unique adaptations. Their snouts act as scent-seeking snorkels or as a grasping tool. Tapirs have an important job in the Amazon rainforest: spreading fungi that helps plants absorb nutrients. The researchers observed tapirs favored roots that were colonized by arbuscular mycorrhizal fungi. Tapirs play a role in the dissemination of fungi spores through their waste. In the rainforest, the colonization of new areas by mycorrhizal fungi results in continued benefits for plants. The sharp senses and tough hides of these nocturnal animals offer little protection against the threats of habitat loss and poaching.

The significance of mycophagous mammals goes beyond mere dining preferences and demands more research. Elliott et al.'s comprehensive study on "Mammalian Mycophagy" delves into the fungi eating habits of various mammals. This study, citing a whopping 1,154 sources over 146 years, identifies 508 mammal species across 15 orders that indulge in fungi. It is worth mentioning that the spores of 58 different fungi species can survive being ingested, demonstrating their remarkable resilience and capacity to disperse without causing harm.

The interplay between mammals and fungi has wide-reaching implications. It's not just about dining preferences; it's about how these interactions shape ecosystems. Mammals' role in dispersing fungal spores influences the evolution of mushrooms, demonstrating the interconnectedness of these species and their impact on global biodiversity. It emphasizes the crucial role fungi play in nourishing a multitude of mammals and maintaining the delicate balance of our environment. It's no wonder why mushrooms adapt to attract mammals.

What if one of these spore-dispersing mammals went extinct? Fungi play an integral role in breaking down matter and recycling nutrients as well as mycorrhizal connections with plants. Within this intricate web, the disappearance of even a single strand could have far-reaching effects. In this chapter, I will explore mammals that consume truffles and their related subterranean fruiting bodies of hypogeous mycorrhizal fungi.

The Remarkable Truffle Hunters

Truffles is the food for kings, gods, and pigs.
~ANTONIO CARLUCCIO,
(Italian chef and restaurateur)

Truffles, those elusive underground delicacies, form a fascinating part of nature's hidden treasures. Often associated with specific trees, these ectomycorrhizal wonders belong to the Ascomycota genus, *Tuber*. But here's a secret: they're not the sole players in the underground mushroom world. Enter false truffles, members of Basidiomycota, a vital food source for many animals. Among them, you'll find the likes of *Rhizopogon* and *Gymnomyces*.

Let's simplify things for now and call all these underground marvels "truffles." Later, we'll dive into the luxurious world of *Tuber* truffles, those cherished by humans. "Hypogeous" is the term that describes these hidden potato-like mushrooms, thriving beneath select tree species. These fungi have devised intriguing ways to spread their spores with the help of animals. Imagine their alluring aroma as nature's irresistible magnet, much like the scent of freshly baked bread.

Whether they are in a European truffle orchard or deep in the forest, critters on a truffle hunt cannot resist the allure of these fragrant scents. Zoochory plays a pivotal role in truffle propagation, aiding spore distribution and nurturing the health of host trees. Let's venture into the world of mammals that relish indulging in these aromatic delights.

Truffle Tales:
The Hidden World of Wild Boars and Fungi

In the heart of lush forests, a powerful wild boar snorts and digs, its tusks gleaming like ivory daggers. The wild boar, *Sus scrofa*, stands as a robust and crafty creature. I once had a memorable encounter with one during a wildlife biology study; this giant charged at me, tusks glinting, a scene from the Cenozoic, the Age of Mammals. Fortunately, he stopped short and vanished into the bush, allowing me to breathe for another day. Like us, these boars savor aromatic truffles, these prized underground delicacies. This unlikely partnership between wild boars and truffles is a fascinating story of ecological give-and-take.

Wild boars, also known as sangliers in some regions, aren't picky eaters. They'll munch on roots, berries, and even small prey when the opportunity arises. The boars seek the intoxicating delights of truffles found beneath the soil. They're like connoisseurs of the underworld, unearthing these culinary gems with their powerful snouts and tireless digging.

The wild boar's relationship with truffles isn't just about consumption. As they forage, their rooting and digging behaviors disrupt the forest floor, affecting plant cover and diversity, even reaching into the critical mycelium layer— the essential fungal network supporting truffle growth. This disruption has led to a decline in truffle production, making these fungi even pricier. It's a double-edged sword: studies have shown that their digging can also stimulate truffle growth and eventually yield bountiful harvests. Research by Piattoni et al., 2016, indicates their digestive enzymes may enhance spore germination, aiding truffle colonization in new habitats.

What makes pigs champions of finding truffles is their amazing sense of smell. According to *Pet Pig World*, pigs can detect odors as deep as 25 feet underground and recognize their scent from 8 to 11 kilometers away! The rustling of leaves and the faint echo of their footsteps signal the pig's presence in the forests as they travel up to 15 kilometers in a single day. These wild boars are long-distance truffle delivery agents. As they munch, poop, and move, they disperse truffle spores throughout the forest, ensuring the fungi's germination and the ability to form ectomycorrhizal connections with trees.

The interplay between wild boars and truffles is not without its challenges. In France, when sanglier populations plummeted from excessive hunting, they resorted to desperate measures. They introduced domestic sows into the wild to mate with the remaining wild boars, leading to a dramatic population explosion. It is worth mentioning that domestic pigs and wild pigs belong to the same species, *Sus scrofa*. This surge impacted both truffle populations and the economic bottom line, given the lucrative truffle business.

What makes truffles irresistible to wild boars? These fungi contain androstenol, a sex hormone found in male pig saliva. I know, it doesn't sound appetizing to me. Produced in the testes and secreted during courtship, this pheromone lures female pigs to truffles, triggering their earth-rooting quest. Truffles possess an intriguing "aphrodisiac" quality, captivating pigs and humans. The idea of truffle pheromones acting as love potions traces back to ancient Greece! Perhaps this notion stemmed from observing the fervent truffle-chasing behavior of pigs. In fact, studies also suggest truffles can stimulate sexual desire in male boars that consume or even sniff truffles. It's a love story written in the language of scent, played out amidst the tangled roots and earth below the forest floor.

In a fascinating turn of events, scientists have discovered that deer truffles, *Elaphomyces granulatus*, which are highly sought after by wild boars, are the primary cause of radioactive cesium contamination in these animals. These creatures, emblematic of the wild and resilient spirit of the forest, carry an invisible burden of radioactivity, the origin of which has long puzzled researchers. Historically, we presumed that the catastrophic Chernobyl nuclear power plant meltdown in 1986 could be the major source of radioactivity in wild boars. The calamity, originating in Ukraine, unleashed a catastrophic release of radioactive material that unfurled its toxic cloak over 40 percent of Europe, extending its reach to parts of Asia, Africa, and North America. The disaster's far-reaching consequences left an indelible mark on the environment, contributing to the radioactivity that lingers in the wild today. But recent research has uncovered a startling revelation. "Environmental Science and Technology" published a study suggesting that fallout from nuclear weapons testing, conducted decades before Chernobyl, remains a significant contributor to the cesium levels found in these creatures.

Radioactive cesium has been a longstanding concern because of its harmful effects on the environment and human health. Scientists measured radioactive cesium levels in various potential food items within the study area, and deer truffles emerged as the dominant source of contamination. These subterranean fungi exhibited contamination levels that exceeded those of edible mushrooms and other food components by an astonishing order of magnitude.

The implications of this discovery are profound. It underscores the lasting legacy of nuclear weapons testing on our environment, as even decades later, the fallout continues to affect the wild inhabitants of our forests. Wild boars bear the brunt of the radioactivity that now taints their populations. Are wild boars our canary in the coalmine for nuclear fallout?

But fear not, truffle lovers! Studies have shown that truffles of the genus *Tuber*, the prized culinary varieties, are free from radioactive contamination. So, you can still indulge in the earthy, luxurious taste of these forest jewels without radioactive worries. Not sure about eating wild boar meat, though. The intertwined tales of wild boars and truffles reveal not just a mutualistic relationship but also the unforeseen consequences of historical human actions in the natural world.

Outsourcing our Sense of Smell to Hunt Truffles

"The power of a bloodhound's nose!" is what seasoned truffle hunters declare when asked about their ultimate superpower wish. Forget fancy lasers or flying. All they crave is the ability to navigate the forest on a nose of unparalleled prowess. Why should we when we can outsource the sense of smell to our trusty companions: dogs and pigs? Among these contenders, pigs have historically stolen the limelight as exemplary truffle seekers. Their snouts, adept at sniffing out buried treasures, were once unparalleled in the world of truffle hunting. With an exceptional olfactory capacity, these porcine detectives could discern the seductive scent of truffles nestled deep beneath the earth. One might ponder if ancient humans first observed wild pigs unearthing these hidden delicacies. Bartolomeo Platina, an Italian Renaissance writer, recorded the use of truffle pigs in the 15th century, marking the commencement of this extraordinary partnership. In 1875, pigs had gained significant value as truffle hunters, and a truffle pig could cost 200 francs, a considerable amount of money back then. However, the sale value of the truffle was worth the cost of the hog.

Nicolas Cage stars as a reclusive truffle hunter who lives deep in the Oregon wilderness in the 2021 film Pig, which pays tribute to this distinctive partnership. His poignant journey takes him back to the bustling city of Portland, where he embarks on a quest to reclaim his cherished truffle pig, stolen from him. Trained truffle pigs are often the target of audacious heists, and sometimes killed to eliminate competition.

However, as history unfolded, a shift occurred, showcasing the emergence of dogs as the favored truffle hunting companions. While pigs boasted an impressive sense of smell, their innate tendencies and size posed challenges. Their penchant for devouring discovered truffles before hunters could intervene and their tendency to disrupt the delicate mycelium network crucial for truffle growth led to concerns about their impact on truffle-rich environments. To ensure the protection of natural truffle habitats, Italy has taken the drastic step toward banning the use of truffle pigs altogether. Skillful handling and training of these animals became imperative to prevent them from indulging in their discoveries and to protect the delicate ecosystem.

In contrast, truffle-hunting dogs are the top choice because of their smaller size, trainability, and minimal impact on the truffle environment. Dogs, our loyal partners in crime-solving and cuddle puddles, boast a sense of smell that puts ours to shame. Dogs possess an extraordinary olfactory system, with an olfactory bulb occupying a significant portion of their brain, rendering their sense of smell thousands of times more sensitive than that of humans. This heightened sense serves various purposes beyond truffle hunting, from search and rescue operations to medical detections, showcasing their versatility and invaluable contributions across multiple fields. Enter the sleek squad of four-legged detectives. Imagine your nose zeroing in on a single truffle buried feet beneath the forest floor. Yeah, that's dog-level sniffing.

Their secret weapon? A brain with a superior olfactory bulb, a structure within the brain dedicated to processing scent information. This specialized scent-processing center is way bigger than ours, packing in a mind-boggling number of odor receptors. We're talking 10,000 to 100,000 times more than us puny humans! Plus, they have a secret aroma decoder called the Jacobson's organ, letting them sniff out scents we wouldn't know existed. This olfactory superpower isn't just for finding fancy fungi. Dogs are our ultimate scent sleuths, employed in search and rescue missions, sniffing out danger like drugs and explosives. Medical alert dogs can be a lifesaving reality. Dogs can detect certain diseases, such as cancer and diabetes, by smelling the subtle chemical changes that occur in a patient's body. The potential of this remarkable skill lies in early disease detection and life-saving interventions.

It's no wonder training a dog to scent for truffles is a breeze. The Lagotto Romagnolo, dubbed the official truffle dog, with its curly coat reminiscent of a poodle, became renowned for its truffle-hunting abilities. Purchasing a Lagotto can be quite pricey, but unnecessary, since any breed or mutt can be trained to hunt truffles. I'm training my fox terrier to find truffles and chanterelles, and why not? Most edible mushrooms have a distinct scent and no need to dig for them. I can always use the extra set of nose and eyes. This foraging partnership opens doors for many possibilities. The prospect of teaching dogs to identify seasonal edible or medicinal mushrooms and even discern dangerous lookalikes is an exciting avenue for exploration.

In the end, Team Dog, our unwavering, loyal canine friend, takes the truffle trophy, leaving the pigs with a snout-full of honorable mentions. So here's to our pawed friends, the ultimate outsourced olfactory assistant, proving once again that the best things in life come with wet noses and wagging tails.

Red-backed vole Truffle Connoisseur

Out of all the animals, the vole is the one that truly captivates me with its incredible knack for underground exploration and its extraordinary ability to sniff out truffles. The red-backed vole (*Clethrionomys gapperi*) is a small rodent that is native to North America and found in forests. I have officially declared it as my favorite rodent. This humble creature serves as an essential truffle eater and fungal spreader in forest ecosystems. The vole can be mistaken as a mouse or even a mole, but let me clarify the difference. Voles, stout and unassuming, sport short tails and round faces. Their fur, a mosaic of earthy tones, blends with their grassy abodes. Field mice possess slender bodies, embellished with long tails, pointed snouts, and large ears. Field mice embrace a diverse menu, relishing seeds, fruits, insects, and the occasional invertebrate delight. Voles prefer a vegan diet of plants and mushrooms.

Voles rhyme with moles, but don't let that confuse you. Despite being mistaken as rodents, moles are part of the group, once known as insectivores. Adapted to underground living, moles have cylindrical bodies with powerful front limbs and claws, giving them a monster movie appearance. As mentioned earlier, mole latrines are cleaned by fungi in exchange for nutrients. Moles feast upon earthworms, insects, and other critters beneath the soil. Moles, ever the enigmatic recluses, seldom grace the world above. Their solitary existence, etched in subterranean secrecy, remains hidden from prying eyes and they are not as adventurous as voles.

Unlike other sleepy critters, voles don't hibernate, and they don't even need a caffeine boost to keep going. Forget circadian rhythms. Voles embrace a life where day merges with night in a blur of scurrying paws and gnawing teeth. Their world is a labyrinth of self-dug tunnels and cozy dens, teeming with adorable, fur-clad progeny. Talk about fast-forwarding life! Females hit adulthood before you can say "mycelium," popping out litters every few weeks while their offspring go from nursing to solid foods in the blink of an eye. But don't get too attached. They live life in the fast lane, sometimes clocking out after just two moonlit months.

Now, buckle up for the real rollercoaster: vole population numbers. These guys throw epic population parties every few years, turning up the dial on density until the landscape buzzes with their tiny forms. Food quality, weather, natural predators, stress levels, and genetic factors all contribute to this captivating vole drama. Every twist and turn contributes to this fascinating show, leaving scientists scratching their heads and ecologists on the edge of their seats. So next time you see a vole-shaped tunnel, remember—you're witnessing a high-octane lifestyle, death, and burrowing brilliance, played out in the subterranean stage beneath your feet. But it's not just their energetic lifestyle that sets them apart.

The red-backed voles' talent for truffle hunting is both fascinating and essential. While humans have cultivated the art of truffle hunting with the help of trained dogs and pigs, the unassuming vole has evolved its own remarkable abilities to unearth these subterranean delicacies. Voles possess a keen sense of smell, which plays a pivotal role in their truffle-hunting abilities. They attune their specialized olfactory receptors to the volatile organic compounds released by truffles, allowing them to pinpoint the location of these hidden delicacies.

Voles have adapted their digging behavior to locate truffles. They use their sharp, chisel-like incisors to burrow through the soil, creating tunnels and pathways as they search for their subterranean prey. Their small size and agility enable them to navigate the intricate underground networks of roots and mycelium, where truffles are most commonly found.

Voles are not solitary creatures in their truffle quest; they often rely on social learning to improve their foraging techniques. Young voles learn from their parents and siblings, acquiring knowledge about the locations and conditions conducive to truffle growth. This social learning enhances their efficiency in finding truffles and contributes to the perpetuation of this remarkable skill within vole populations.

Voles are crucial in the life cycle of truffles. Their contribution hinges on two key adaptations: spore resilience and in providing a nutrient boost. Encased in a sturdy coat, truffle spores remain unaffected by the vole's digestive enzymes and acidic stomach. This ensures their safe passage through the gastrointestinal tract. Upon exiting the vole, spores become mixed with nutrient-rich feces, creating an ideal microenvironment for germination and subsequent mycelium growth. This dynamic benefits both parties. Voles gain a nutritious meal, while truffles gain efficient spore dispersal and potential colonization of new tree roots through mycorrhizal associations.

Voles' truffle-dispersal activities have broader ecological implications. They influence the survival and growth rates of many tree species by fostering vital mycorrhizal partnerships. Additionally, voles serve as a crucial prey for various predators, playing a key role in the food chain.

In the grand forest theater, voles are the backstage crew, working to ensure the show goes on. Their presence benefits many tree species, all while being an integral part of the food chain. Hawks, owls, snakes, weasels, raccoons, foxes, opossums, and house cats all applaud the voles for their role as a tasty snack.

North American Flying Squirrels

Glaucomys sabrinus: Guardians of the Forest Fungi

Mushrooms, though not a primary source of food, can still benefit mammals. Mushrooms are a nutrient-packed food, offering proteins, Vitamin D, potassium, phosphorus, and selenium, all crucial for bodily functions. Fungi also provide fiber to maintain a healthy digestive system. It's no wonder so many mammals munch on mushrooms. Bears, chipmunks, elk, gophers, marmots, mice, mountain goats, opossums, raccoons, squirrels, shrews, skunks, foxes and many other mammalian species found in North America partake in the consumption of mushrooms. However, we are going to focus on one superstar fungivore.

Meet *Glaucomys sabrinus*, the northern flying squirrel—an enchanting creature that maneuvers through the treetops, defying gravity with its controlled glides. The name "flying squirrel" is a misnomer. Instead of true flight, they execute controlled glides with the help of their patagium—a stretch of skin that extends from wrist to ankle. This evolutionary adaptation allows them to move from one tree to another, navigating the forest canopy with ease. With their laterally flattened tails acting as rudders, flying squirrels exhibit remarkable agility as they gracefully glide through the trees. These enchanting creatures can glide for distances up to 40 meters (130 feet), proving their expertise in the air.

The northern flying squirrel is a charismatic representative of the genus *Glaucomys*, a name that means "gray mouse." Yet, this unassuming name belies the extraordinary abilities and ecological importance as guardian of forest fungi. Amidst the northern forests, the flying squirrel forges a unique connection with mushrooms and truffles, forming the cornerstone of its diet. The captivating fragrance emitted by hypogeous mycorrhizal fungi lures flying squirrels, guiding them to hidden treasures beneath the forest floor.

While they may appear to be agile in the trees, on the ground is a perilous place for flying squirrels. Down there, they face formidable predators, including owls, foxes, martens, and other mammals. Although the risk is high, these remarkable squirrels venture down from their arboreal haven to forage for a diverse diet that includes nuts, acorns, berries, insects, eggs, and even nestling birds, depending on the season. Their adaptability and resourcefulness ensures survival in the face of challenges. The relationship between predator and prey involves a delicate dance, where squirrels consume these fungi and serve as the agents for mycorrhizal spore dispersal. The significance of this relationship extends far beyond the squirrels' treetop domain.

Their role as the experts in the art of zoochory is critical, especially for the health of mycorrhizal fungi. As flying squirrels roam the forest floor in search of their fungal feasts, they disperse the spores in their droppings, facilitating the growth of these vital fungi in different parts of the forest. Mycorrhizal fungi play a crucial role in nutrient and water uptake by various coniferous tree species, enhancing the resilience of the forest ecosystem to climate change.

While the Pacific Northwest takes center stage in this ecological ballet, we can observe the interdependent relationship between flying squirrels and fungi elsewhere as well. From the rugged terrain of Alaska to the lush woodlands of eastern North America, and even the heart of Wisconsin, the northern flying squirrel continues its vital role as a fungal courier. In the hushed whispers of the woods, this partnership knows no geographic bounds. Recognized as a "keystone species" in the Pacific Northwest, it serves as a primary food source for the federally endangered spotted owl (*Strix occidentalis*). A key player in the ecosystem, the northern flying squirrel upholds the delicate balance of nature, ensuring the survival of countless species that rely on its actions. Understanding the flying squirrel's reproductive cycles, habits, and habitat needs are critical to safeguard them from extinction.

Mating occurs in the spring, leading to the birth of two to three pups between May and July. These furry newborns, born naked with a membrane covering their eyes and ears, rely on their mother's care and nourishment. Weaning takes about two months, but the young may stay with their mother for several additional months, learning the ropes of forest life.

While the northern flying squirrel does not hibernate, it adapts to the colder months by reducing its time outside the nest. This creature is nocturnal, displaying two distinct periods of activity each day—one at sunset and another in the early morning. Inclement weather may delay their foraging excursions, but it rarely deters them from their essential tasks.

In a world where forested habitats are disappearing at an alarming rate, the northern flying squirrel faces one of its greatest threats—loss of suitable habitat. These creatures depend on the presence of conifers and older-forest characteristics. Their presence sustains the delicate balance of these ecosystems, ensuring the survival of species that depend on them for sustenance.

In the heart of the northern forests, *Glaucomys sabrinus* continues to glide through the night, guarding the secrets of the forest fungi. Their ecological importance as mycophagists and seed dispersers is an invaluable thread in the intricate web of life that sustains our planet's ecosystems. The northern flying squirrel is a testament to the wonders of nature, proving that even the smallest of creatures can play a monumental role in preserving the delicate balance of our world.

So, next time you hear the rustle of leaves in the twilight, remember the flying squirrel, gliding not just through the trees, but through the very essence of our forests. Let its whispers carry a message of hope, urging us to support conservation efforts to ensure their survival.

Truffle Hunters from Down Under

A Pocket Full of Spores

We should not forget about marsupials found in Australia and Tasmania and their role in mycophagy. Let's start with the Eastern bettong, *Bettongia gaimardi*, and its passion for truffles. Also known as the rat-kangaroo, this unique marsupial boasts a crucial relationship with these subterranean delicacies, forming a mutualistic bond that's more intricate than meets the eye. In fact, eighty percent of a bettong's diet is these pungent prizes.

Picture this: lush woodlands and grasslands of Tasmania, where the Eastern Bettong roams under the cover of night, embarking on a quest for the prized truffles. These secretive underground treasures hold a distinctive taste that the bettongs can't resist. Equipped with an extraordinary sense of smell, they can detect truffle aromas buried up to a foot below the ground—a skill that guides their nightly excavation.

Not only do they rely on their nose, but their paws act like tiny shovels, equipped with long, sharp claws to unearth the hidden treasure. Whiskers, like delicate subterranean antennae, twitch and tremble, guiding them to the elusive truffle bounty. But it's not just about the meal; these creatures play a pivotal role in the forest's health. Truffle feasts transform rat kangaroos into unwitting couriers, their guts acting as armored caravans for precious fungal spores. They deliver these treasures across forest floors, planting the spores in droppings that birth a new generation of truffles.

Yet, this important truffle spore disperser faces a looming threat. Habitat loss and hungry predators like foxes are pushing these marsupial foragers towards extinction. And it's not just the Eastern Bettong—other marsupials like the Burrowing Bettong and Eastern Barred Bandicoot also play crucial roles in the truffle's lifecycle. Their presence in the ecosystem aids in the propagation and growth of these fascinating fungi, emphasizing the collective effort required to maintain the health of the native forests.

Conserving and protecting these endangered marsupials and their habitat is crucial for their survival. The marsupial and its truffle food are essential components of a thriving forest ecosystem.

Potoroos: The Endangered Fungivores

Deep within the emerald embrace of Australian rain-forests, two charismatic marsupials, Gilbert's potoroo (*Potorous gilbertii*) and the Long-footed potoroo (*Potorous longipes*) lead lives unlike any other. Forget hopping after grass—these creatures are obligate fungivores, meaning their survival hinges on a hidden feast beneath the forest floor—truffles and their fungal kin.

The Gilbert's potoroo scurries through the under-growth, a dainty explorer clad in a cloak of soft, brown-gray fur that blends with the dappled sunlight and earthy tones of the ground litter. Its anteater-like snout twitches and probes, sniffing out hidden treasures in the leaf litter with an unerring sense of smell. Its formidable fore-paws, armed with three dagger-like claws, rip through the soil like miniature jackhammers, unearthing fragrant truffles. Sized like a large rabbit, these potoroos measure 12 to 16 inches long, packing a lot of charm in their compact frame.

The Long-footed potoroo, presents a whimsical sight. Its oversized feet, nearly as long as its head, transform it into a living cartoon, hopping through the dappled forest light like a furry wind-up toy. Imagine Bambi's clumsiness combined with a kangaroo's grace, each leap punctuated by the gentle thud of those comical feet. Their fur, a grizzled tapestry of grays and browns, blends with the forest floor, a camouflage fit for avoiding predators. The Long-footed potoroo shares the Gilbert's potoroo's razor-sharp claws, ready to shred through earth like miniature excavators. But instead of a long, sniffing proboscis, it sports a snub button nose for poking about in leaf litter. And while it towers over its cousin, reaching 16 inches, its charm stays firmly in place.

Both species possess captivating, curious eyes and sharp senses of smell, essential for navigating their hidden fungal feasts in the forest. With long, adaptable tails aiding in balance and maneuvering, these marsupials are remarkable in their exploration of their woodland homes.

The renowned Australian naturalist John Gilbert lends his name to Gilbert's Potoroo, the pint-sized kangaroo lookalike. Found only in the wilds of Tasmania, these rare creatures dedicate their lives to sniffing out over 30 species of hypogeous fungi, making up a whopping 90% of their diet. Above-ground fruiting bodies make up a small amount of what they consume.

Their skill is almost surgical, leaving behind a trail of neat, cone-shaped holes—silent testaments to their fungal digging. After digesting its fungal haul, it scatters spores like confetti, ensuring the fungi's continued reign and maintaining the delicate balance of the forest ecosystem.

Sadly, for this truffle-loving marsupial, it's the most endangered marsupial, its survival hanging by a thread. Threats include wildfires, non-native predators like cats and foxes, genetic diversity loss, and climate change. Loss or degradation of the plants that host their fungi adds to their struggles. Efforts to ensure their survival include relocating a handful to protected areas in South Australia, with the population estimated at around 100 individuals by 2022. Their fate is a stark reminder of the fragility of nature's balance.

Now, let's shift our attention to the Long-footed potoroo, *Potorous longipes*, restricted to the coastal border between New South Wales and Victoria. Long-footed potoroos can devour around 58 different fungal types, including truffles, thanks to their shearing premolars and molars designed for a varied menu. Their dietary contributions are diverse, occasionally incorporating fruits, plant materials, and even soil-dwelling invertebrates. But even its diverse palate can't outrun the threats of introduced predators and logging encroaching on its limited range.

Similar to Gilbert's potoroo, the Long-footed potoroos play a crucial role in the symbiotic relationship between mycorrhizal fungi and trees. These Potoroos are two extraordinary marsupials that have evolved to depend on fungi for their survival. Both exhibit a profound connection with the subterranean fungal diet as they contribute to forest well-being through the dispersal of spores.

The plight of the Gilbert's and Long-footed potoroos is a call to action. Conservation efforts are underway, but their fate hangs in the balance. By amplifying their story and protecting their dwindling homes, we can ensure these fungivores continue their essential part in the emerald shadows of the South Australia wilds. So, the next time you forage for mushrooms, spare a thought for these hidden heroes from Down Under. They may be small, but their role in the environment is anything but.

Chapter 10

Mushroom Munching Monkeys

> *One of the basic steps in saving a threatened*
> *species is to learn more about it: its diet, its*
> *mating and reproductive processes, its range*
> *patterns, its social behavior.*
>
> ~DIAN FOSSEY

Mycology resounds with a curious tale seldom told—a narrative woven in the secretive, fungi-feasting habits of primates. Venture into the rainforests' lush heartlands or other remote regions, and witness a shared fungal fondness between our kind and fellow primates—a bond etched deep into our evolutionary past. Join me as we unravel the intriguing world of primate mycophagy, exploring its ecological significance and delving into the lives of select primate species.

Primates, such as humans, bonobos, and gorillas, have a diverse diet that includes mushrooms. About 22 primate species consume fungi, with some devoting a significant part of their day to this unique food choice (Hanson et al., 2003).

Let's start our journey with the petite mycophagous wonder, the Buffy-tufted marmoset *Callithrix aurita*. With its ghoulish appearance, this monkey, no bigger than a squirrel, could be an extra in a Tim Burton film. This marmoset sports dark Gothic makeup over a white face, with a long black fur coat and white tufted ears. The locals call this primate "sagui-caveirinha," which translates to "little skull marmoset" in Portuguese. But beneath this whimsical goth costume beats the heart of a true fungi fanatic. Devoting a whopping 12% of its day to consuming fungi, the buffy-tufted marmoset holds the title of the smallest mycophagous primate.

Nestled within the Atlantic rainforest biome of South-Eastern Brazil, this marmoset thrives amidst a treasure trove of fungal diversity. While these marmosets relish insects and fruits, mushrooms stand tall as a crucial supplementary food source. Laden with vital nutrients and minerals, these fungi contribute to their overall vitality. By indulging in these fungal feasts, marmosets play a pivotal role in spore dispersal.

Alas, the International Union for Conservation of Nature (IUCN) has cast a grim spotlight on the Buffy-tufted marmoset, listing it among the top 25 most endangered primate species worldwide. As the marmoset's habitat contends with the relentless challenges of deforestation, urban sprawl, and human incursion, the rich variety of mushrooms they rely upon faces a dire threat. The ecological trinity of Fauna, Flora, and Funga connection bears immense importance. We must support the cause of conservation, nurturing hope for the survival of this endearing marmoset and its cherished mushrooms.

Next, let's showcase Goeldi's marmoset, *Callimico goeldii*, another fascinating example of primate mycophagy. These marmosets call the upper Amazon basin in Bolivia, Brazil, Colombia, and Peru their home. These squirrel-sized primates boast a fur coat that varies in color and texture, making them stand out in their lush, rainforest habitat. Most commonly draped in shades of black, Goeldi's monkeys boast a spectrum of fur hues, ranging from deep blacks to dark browns, reddish tones, and silvery browns. Some even rock a jet-black appearance. Their diverse fur colors add an air of mystery, ensuring each monkey stands out in its unique way.

But what truly captivates the eye is their regal flair—adult Goeldi's monkeys sport a splendid, flowing mane cascading from their necks, lending them an almost royal air amid the foliage. You might spot some with highlights of red or silver in their 'crown' of poofy hair, while others sport white streaks on their faces or torsos. A select few might even exhibit lighter-colored rings at the base of their tails, a remarkable aspect of their appearance. Amidst this luxurious fur, their faces stand out—dark, bare, and expressive, highlighting their emotions amidst the furry backdrop.

Their grooming habits are equally distinctive. These primates have claws on their toes, save for the second toe, referred to as the "toilet claw"—a term that might seem peculiar given its function in grooming. I'd rather call it a "grooming claw" to avoid any potty connotations! This specialized nail allows them to clean and maintain the appearance of their fur. What primate doesn't want to look good?

In the bustling understory of tropical rainforests, these elusive creatures dedicate a staggering 63% of their feeding time to foraging for specific fungal species. They possess a refined taste for fungi like *Auricularia auricula* (wood ears), *Auricularia mesenterica, Ascopolyporus polyporoides,* and *Ascopolyporus polychrous*—consuming three times more fungi than the average human. The genus *Ascopolyporus* are bulbous to hoof-shaped, in resemblance to various polypores or shelf fungi.

What is mind-boggling is that Goeldi's monkeys lack the usual digestive tools or foregut fermentation for tackling fungi, yet they gobble them down with gusto, prompting scientists to speculate about undiscovered adaptations aiding their digestion of fungal sporocarps. One plausible explanation is that fungi provide essential vitamins and minerals. Or even offer medicinal curatives. Because of the ample mushrooms, there's less competition for fruits. These monkeys consume fungi throughout the year, with a notable increase during the early dry season when fruits become scarcer. Researchers have proposed that the reliance on low-nutrient fungi may contribute to Goeldi's monkeys' lower population density and larger home ranges compared to other monkeys of similar size in the same forest. The Goeldi monkeys' hidden adaptation for digesting fungal sporocarps is a mystery begging to be unraveled. A thorough understanding of the monkeys' physiology is essential and warrants further investigation. Investigating how Goeldi monkeys digest nutrient-poor fungi could lead to the discovery of novel digestive pathways. This research might yield potent enzymes and gut microbes, arming us with new weapons against human digestive disorders and perhaps fortify our immune system. Imagine a future where understanding their digestive processes contributes to broader therapeutic strategies.

A Word on Lichens and the Yunnan Snub-Nosed Monkey

Let's delve into the captivating realm of lichens, those remarkable organisms born from the intricate symbiosis between algae or cyanobacteria and diverse fungal species. Thriving in extreme conditions, from polar freezes to arid deserts, lichens play a crucial role as environmental sentinels, assessing air quality and providing sustenance to a myriad of creatures. Lichens serve as both habitat and camouflage for invertebrates, concealing themselves in lichen-covered landscapes. Birds, too, incorporate these tiny wonders into their lives, using them as nesting materials. The Olive-headed weaver in Madagascar takes it a step further, constructing its entire nest from a specific lichen species within the *Usnea* genus.

For herbivores like caribou and reindeer, lichens act as a lifeline, constituting up to 90% of their winter diet. These animals possess an extraordinary ability to smell lichens beneath layers of snow. *Cladina stellaris,* in particular, is a lichen species that is devoured with relish. However, it's not limited to just caribou and reindeer. In southeastern Alaska, mountain goats rely on lichens like *Lobaria linita* as a food source to sustain themselves during periods of snow-covered vegetation. These lichens, including species of *Bryoria* and *Alectoria*, often grow on trees, providing an additional source of nutrition.

Enter our star lichen-consuming primate, the Yunnan snub-nosed monkey, *Rhinopithecus bieti,* an endangered species found in the Yunnan Province of China. In the province, their specific habitat is the Yunling mountain range in northwestern Yunnan and southeastern Tibet. This unique monkey has earned the nickname "Yunnan golden hair monkey" and "black-and-white snub-nosed monkey" because of its distinctive appearance, which combines a fluffy coat, plump pink lips, a Buddha belly and a surprised facial expression with mere slits of a nose lacking nasal bones.

But beyond its charming looks, the Yunnan monkey with a flattened nose possesses an equally fascinating and unexpected passion—a penchant for lichen. They consume *Bryoria* species, referred to as the horsehair lichens, because of their slender and hanging nature. You can find *Bryoria* clinging to conifers and scattered across the tundra soil. Forget fancy fruits. Snub-nosed monkeys munch on "horsehair lichens" that dangle from trees like long strands of dry spinach. And they're not shy about it—these monkeys spend a jaw-dropping 95% of their mealtime slurping down the lichen.

During the warmer months, these monkeys embark on extensive journeys in search of diverse food sources. They thrive in the rugged terrain. Resting on rocky outcrops offers them both an advantage in spotting predators and a source of warmth during the winter months. Similar to other primates, they are omnivorous and adaptable. However, in harsh winters with limited food, they rely on lichens as their primary source of nourishment. Lichen-eating is a rare behavior among primates, and the Yunnan snub-nosed monkey is one of the few species that partake in this behavior. Their stomachs possess a remarkable ability to extract nutrients from these protein-poor and toxic lichens that are laden with indigestible carbohydrates.

The future of the Yunnan snub-nosed monkey is fraught with challenges. Their population decline has led to their current classification as "endangered." The unique ecological niche and habitat of these monkeys make them vulnerable to changes in the environment. Habitat loss and human activities further compound the challenges they face. Ongoing conservation efforts strive to safeguard their population, ensuring the survival of this extraordinary species for future generations.

Bonobos: The Truffle-Loving Hippies of the Jungle

Baby bonobos refuse to survive without the mother—they have only one goal—to die, because they cannot live without love."
~CLAUDINE ANDRÉ, Conservationist
and Founder of Lola ya Bonobo Sanctuary

Nestled deep within the lush emerald maze of the Democratic Republic of Congo, a captivating tale unfolds—a secret society of gourmands, the bonobos. These enigmatic great apes, our closest kin, have an unexpected penchant for truffles. These aren't your average apes, grunting and brawling over scraps. They're the bonobos, the elegant swingers with a penchant for peace, love, and gourmet fungi.

Bonobos, often referred to as the 'Make Love, Not War' apes, are the elegant simians of the jungle. They are smaller and leaner compared to their chimpanzee cousins. Their bodies are slim and dark, featuring pink lips and hair that parts on their heads. Their most human-like trait is their notably long limbs, setting them apart from other apes. These graceful acrobats can walk on two legs, resembling early hominids in their upright gait.

Now, consider the robust chimpanzees, dark and bulkier, with a penchant for territorial displays and hierarchical societies led by alpha males. In their world, survival hinges on strength and cunning. Gorillas, the gentle giants, dwarf their cousins in size, living in familial units led by a dominant silverback male. Their survival secret lies in herbivory and conflict resolution through intimidation. Chimpanzees and gorillas occasionally consume mushrooms, whereas bonobos forage for subterranean fungi.

Bonobos live life with an ethos of peace and harmony. Unlike their more aggressive chimpanzee cousins, their society stands out for its remarkable egalitarian structure, rooted in female-centered relationships. Forget the alpha-male drama—love reigns supreme, with conflict resolved in a flurry of embraces rather than fists. Perhaps this explains their absence in the movie, *Planet of the Apes*.

Another fact that makes bonobos stand out is their repertoire of sexual activities, which extend far beyond reproduction and would make the Kama Sutra blush. For bonobos, sex is a multi-tool that builds bridges, soothes ruffled feathers, and even keeps the peace better than any bullying dominance. Age, gender, solo acts, or family affairs —none exist in the free-spirited realm of their amorous adventures. So, if you're looking for a society where a playful wink speaks volumes, take a peek into the world of the bonobos, where every day is a sensual celebration of life and every touch tells a story.

Enter *Hysterangium bonobo*, a truffle named in honor

of these discerning apes. Alexander Georgiev, a dedicated primatologist, stumbled upon this truffle-loving behavior in the Kokolopori Bonobo Reserve. This serendipitous encounter revealed not only the affection bonobos have for truffles but also an undiscovered fungal species. Led by their astute noses, bonobos could detect the faint aroma of the truffle wafting through the air or by digging into the soil and, like a culinary expert, take a whiff from their fingertips. Their gastronomic delight and innate ability to forage for these truffles that brought *Hysterangium bonobo* into the limelight.

But what makes *H. bonobo* so appealing, not only to bonobos but to us as well? The truffle has a fascinating secret. It has tiny crystal-coated filaments that work as both defense and scent dispersal. The truffle's adaptation is remarkable, suggesting that it has more to offer than meets the eye. Its fragrance, rivaling the finest culinary delights, *H. bonobo* secures a special place in the hearts of discerning apes.

Hysterangium bonobo is no mere snack; it plays a vital role in the bonobos' diet and the Congo ecosystem. Rich in nutrients, its microscopic spores survive the digestive tract, hinting at potential appeal beyond the forest. Yes, this discovered truffle might be of culinary value to humans. The exploration of primate mycophagy, the consumption of fungi, unravels the intricate relationships between primates and fungi across various ecosystems.

While biologists have made significant strides in researching primate mycophagy, there is still a vast amount of knowledge to be gained regarding this behavior. Researchers have used various methods, such as stomach content analysis, direct observation, and fecal analysis, to study mycophagy among primates. Incorporating DNA analysis and stable isotope analysis into future research may reveal deeper insights into the specific fungal species consumed by different primate species.

But why do primates, like bonobos, dedicate substantial portions of their lives to fungi? Mycophagy might be a clever strategy to decrease competition for food during dry seasons, accessing a nutrient-rich source others overlook. It influences home range size and distribution patterns, potentially reducing conflicts among neighboring groups. Or can fungi provide medicinal value, another interesting connection to be addressed in the next chapter?

Primate mycophagy, a fascinating and ancient phenomenon, offers a glimpse into the intricate web of relationships that connect these intelligent creatures with the fungal world. From Goeldi's monkeys in South America to the elusive Black snub-nosed monkeys in China, these primates have shown us that mushrooms and fungi are more than just food; they are an integral part of their lives and the ecosystems they inhabit.

Beyond individual animals, primate mycophagy has far-reaching effects. The dispersal of fungal spores in primate dung contributes to the health and vitality of forest ecosystems. Understanding primate mycophagy, a window to our past as hunter-gatherers, brings us closer to deciphering the intricate web of relationships that connect intelligent creatures with the fungal world—a revelation that continues to unfold in the heart of Earth's most vibrant landscapes.

Chapter 11

Nature Apothecaries: Animals that seek medicinal mushrooms

It seemed to me so completely wrong, this acceptance of inevitable disease: why should all domestic animals, as well as human children, be so afflicted with disease, while other creatures— for example, wild birds—remain almost totally immune?

~JULIETTE DE BAIRACLI LEVY,
Herbalist/Healer

Let's explore the captivating world of animals and their quest for medicinal mushrooms—a phenomenon that mirrors our own pursuit of health and well-being. In 1978, biologist Daniel Janzen made an astonishing proposition. He proposed herbivores weren't just munching leaves— they were strategically targeting plants rich in secondary metabolites, chemical compounds with surprising health benefits. This opened a new frontier in biology, where animals became the ultimate biohackers. Coined in 1993, the term zoopharmacognosy, a tongue-twisting fusion of *zoo* (animal), *pharma* (drug), and *gnosy* (knowing), emerged as a new field in biology. The term gained popularity through academic works and a book by Cindy Engel, *Wild Health: How Animals Keep Themselves Well and What We Can Learn from Them*. The bulk of the research has been on animals and plants. Animals eat charcoal and clay for their medicinal benefits, despite lacking nutrition. Charcoal and clay can remove toxic alkaloids from a variety of consumed foods. Yet one of the most intriguing aspects of zoopharmacognosy is the role fungi play in animal health. The idea of animals self-medicating with fungi is revolutionary, and opened the door to new research for the astute mycologist.

Zoopharmacognosy is similar to ethnomycology, the anthropological study of how human cultures interact with fungi, from ancient rituals to modern medicine. Animals, through their natural behaviors, may also identify and use fungi with medicinal benefits that we have overlooked. Observing these behaviors can lead to the discovery of new therapeutic compounds. It's important to note that life-saving fungal medicines for cancer and other diseases could be lost if we don't protect threatened habitats. My motto centers on the belief that nature offers effective remedies long before rigorous laboratory testing can validate their efficacy.

The mechanisms behind how animals identify and use medicinal mushrooms remain a subject of ongoing research. Visual and olfactory cues, such as mushroom color, shape, or scent, may guide them. Bioactive compounds like polysaccharides, triterpenes, and polyphenols found in mushrooms possess potent pharmacological activities, offering anti-inflammatory, antimicrobial, and antitumor effects.

Mushrooms, a nutritional powerhouse, provide animals with vitamins, minerals, and antioxidants. UV-exposed mushrooms are a source of Vitamin D crucial for bone and immune health, while minerals like selenium, copper, magnesium, and phosphorus contribute to overall well-being. Animals consuming mushrooms may experience immune system enhancement, infection fighting, reduced inflammation, improved digestion, and even protection against parasites. Fungi can help animals recover from different ailments. The discovery of animals using mushrooms for self-medication has significant implications for our health. Animals have a natural knowledge of the healing properties of plants and fungi, which might hold valuable insights overlooked by society. Studying their behavior could unlock the development of new medicines and therapies. The phenomenon of animal self-medication with mushrooms highlights the intricate and fascinating relationship between animals and their natural environment. Further research into this area holds immense potential for saving endangered animals. As noted earlier, Paul Stamets did research on how extracts from tinder mushrooms and reishi can help bees against viral infection.

Highlighting this phenomenon, anecdotes and documented accounts abound. Amazon rainforest primates, Siberian reindeer, and chimpanzees in Tanzania showcase distinct preferences for certain mushrooms to address specific health concerns. One of the most interesting examples of animal self-medication with mushrooms is the behavior of chimpanzees in the Mahale Mountains of Tanzania. When suffering from intestinal parasites, chimpanzees exhibit a distinct preference for consuming the fruiting bodies of the mushroom *Phellinus igniarius*, the Willow Bracket, a white rot fungus. Researchers have also observed chimpanzees in Gombe National Park, Tanzania, eating the reishi mushroom, which is known for its anti-inflammatory and immune-enhancing properties. Diane Fossey observed gorillas in Rwanda munching on *Ganoderma applanatum*, a hard leather tough polypore growing on trees, also known as the artist conk. Highland gorillas seek medicinal mushrooms, especially *Ganoderma applanatum*. This massive mushroom poses challenges when dislodging it from trees. Young gorillas have a hard time reaching it, but older gorillas carry it for several hundred feet and protect it from other gorillas.

Grifola frondosa, or maitake mushrooms, are a favorite food of deer in the rolling meadows of Europe. Maitake mushrooms exhibit anti-inflammatory properties. Maintaining strong immune systems is crucial for deer, as they are prey animals and need to stay healthy and disease-free. Bears consume maitake mushrooms as well. People have observed bears chomping on *Inonotus obliquus*, chaga mushrooms, which are packed with antioxidants. Chaga mushrooms are renowned for their cell-protecting and immune-boosting abilities. Chaga mushrooms may help bears stay healthy during their long hibernation periods. There hasn't been serious research on the bear chaga connection and might be a well worth studying project. So, grab your hiking boots and a healthy dose of curiosity. The next time you see a critter chewing on a peculiar fungus, pay attention—you might observe a lesson in natural medicine. The animal apothecary awaits!

What Elephants Can Teach Us
About Medicinal Mushrooms

In the enchanting forests of the southern Cape, South Africa, a captivating story unfolds—one of survival, adaptation, and the hidden wonders within the majestic Knysna elephants. Once on the brink of extinction because of the relentless ivory trade, these gentle giants have not only defied the odds but have also unveiled a mesmerizing aspect of their existence: the intentional use of the medicinal polypore, *Ganoderma applanatum*.

Boasting medicinal properties, *Ganoderma applanatum*, the "Artist's Conk" or "Red Mother Fungus," has earned its acclaim. Packed with steroidal compounds and renowned for its immunostimulating effects, this fungus is a nutritional treasure trove, boasting B-complex vitamins, pantothenic acids, phosphorus, iron, calcium, selenium, potassium, and sodium. In China, it's prized for its therapeutic potential in treating conditions like rheumatic tuberculosis and esophageal cancer. Chinese traditional medicine reveres the related species, *Ganoderma lucidum*, or reishi, as the longevity mushroom.

The revelation about the Knysna elephants and their preference for *Ganoderma applanatum* stems from the meticulous observations of biologist and elephant researcher Gareth Patterson. Over two decades, Patterson has delved into the behaviors of these southernmost forest elephants, adapting to the challenging environment they roam. Through dung sample analysis, Patterson discovered that fifty percent of the matter contained traces of *Ganoderma applanatum*, confirmed by mycologists.

"I made this discovery in the early 2000s while undertaking research on the world's most southerly free-roaming elephants—a highly endangered relict population—the very elusive Knysna elephants of the southern Cape, South Africa," Patterson explains. His findings opened an extraordinary chapter in elephant behavior, showcasing a species feeding on medicinal mushrooms for self-medication.

The elephants' colossal brick-like molars, powerful enough to break through the tough bracket mushroom, demonstrate their deliberate choice of *Ganoderma applanatum*. Unraveling the mystery of their diet, DNA analysis of dung revealed that elephants seek and consume G. applanatum rather than by chance. Deeper still, confirming the deliberate quest by elephants for the fungus as a nutritional supplement. This behavior is not exclusive to the Knysna elephants alone. Southern Africa is home to over 1500 mushroom species, including *Ganoderma*, which is valued for its medicinal properties by both elephants and traditional healers. In Zimbabwe, practitioners have long incorporated *Ganoderma* into their holistic health practices, acknowledging its antiviral, antibacterial, and antiparasitic properties.

The echoes of the elephants' wisdom extend beyond South African borders. In Kenya, locals use elephant dung for medicinal applications containing *Ganoderma*, highlighting the interdependence between animals and the natural pharmacopeia around them. Trumpeting wisdom, the Knysna elephants weave lessons of adaptation and inherent knowledge encoded within the natural world. Nature's pharmacy heals even the mightiest beings.

Sloth Fur: A Hidden Hotspot
for Medical Miracles?

In the lush canopies of Central and South American rainforests, where the air hums with life and verdant foliage stretches as far as the eye can see, resides one of the most enigmatic creatures of the natural world: the sloth. These slow-moving mammals, with their squished faces, long claws, and scruffy fur, capture the imagination of many. Sloths have such a slow metabolism that they poop only once a week. Their adorable appearance hides a fascinating story of ecological importance and potential medical significance. This story involves their mutually beneficial relationship with fungi.

Sloths, specifically the three-toed variety (*Bradypus variegatus*), are denizens of the treetops, spending most of their lives nestled amidst the branches of towering rainforest giants. Their fur transforms into a thriving ecosystem all on its own.

The coat of the sloth is a marvel of nature, comprising two distinct layers: a soft inner layer close to the skin, and a longer, coarser outer layer riddled with tiny cracks and crevices. In these microhabitats a diverse array of life finds refuge, including green algae, fungi, bacteria, roundworms, cockroaches, other insects, and caterpillars. It's fascinating to observe that once the sloth has completed its bowel movement, mature moths seize the chance to deposit their eggs on the feces, leading to the emergence of larvae that feed on the excrement. Say goodbye to the hassle of carrying around pooper-scoopers when walking a sloth.

Among the inhabitants of sloth fur, fungi have emerged as intriguing subjects of study. Recent research has revealed that the hair of three-toed sloths in Panama serves as a rich reservoir of bioactive fungi, capable of producing compounds with potent anti-parasitic, anti-cancer, and anti-bacterial properties. This discovery opens a window into an unexplored realm of potential therapeutic agents, offering hope for the development of new treatments for diseases such as malaria, Chagas disease, and certain types of cancer. It's like a tiny pharmacy growing right on the sloth's back.

The presence of fungi in sloth fur raises intriguing questions about the relationship between these organisms and their mammalian hosts. While it remains unclear how fungi come to inhabit sloth fur, researchers speculate that they may have a symbiotic relationship with other organisms present in the ecosystem, such as the green algae found on sloth hair. This intricate web of interactions underscores the interconnectedness of life within the rainforest and highlights the importance of biodiversity in maintaining ecosystem health. This "fur-ocious" ecosystem is a mystery waiting to be unraveled. It's a whole interconnected world up there in the rainforest canopy!

Studies conducted on sloth populations in rehabilitation centers and sanctuaries have provided valuable insights into the microbial communities inhabiting sloth fur. Researchers have identified many candidate microorganisms with the potential to yield novel therapeutic compounds, offering a glimmer of hope in the fight against antibiotic resistance—a looming global health crisis.

As researchers continue to unravel the mysteries of this complex ecosystem, they shed light on the intricate relationships that sustain biodiversity and offer new avenues for exploration in the quest for medical breakthroughs. In the end, the humble sloth emerges not only as an emblem of leisurely existence but also as a silent guardian of the rainforest, harboring secrets that may hold the key to unlocking some incredible medical breakthroughs!

Chapter 12

Drunk and/or Stoned on Fungi

*There is a world beyond ours, a world
that is far away, nearby and invisible.*
~ Maria Sabina

Nature's stage overflows with captivating animal behaviors that challenge our understanding. Do animals accidentally get intoxicated while searching for high-calorie foods? Or do animals enjoy getting inebriated or high on fungus? Is random chance responsible for getting drunk or high? Before we jump into the popular psilocybin mushrooms and beautiful *Amanita muscaria* species, let's look at the number one producer of ethanol and inebriation, yeasts. We have all seen those drunken robins and tipsy squirrels. Not to mention our own attraction to alcoholic products. From beer and wine, to hard liquor, we primates are not shy about enjoying an occasional inebriated state. Unfortunately, alcohol is the most commonly abused substance worldwide. Let's delve into nature's brewery and her customers.

The "drunken monkey" hypothesis, posited by Robert Dudley, suggests ancestral human encounters with small amounts of alcohol derived from fermented fruits and nectars. According to a 2019 study, the fermentation process in ethanol production not only provides supplementary nutrients but also creates subtle neurological incentives for individuals to seek energy-rich sustenance. I will delve into the intricate relationship between wild yeasts, their production of ethanol through fermentation, and the responses elicited from diverse fauna encountering these intoxicating floral brews.

Tipsy Tales: Wild Yeast, Fermentation, and Nature's Intoxicated Critters

In the enchanting world of nature's hidden mysteries, a microscopic revolution is brewing. It's a tale of wild yeasts—unicellular fungi dwelling within nectar—transforming serene floral landscapes into mini-fermentation zones. And ripe fruits into nature's bar and wine cellars. This alchemical process, much like brewing, produces ethereal scents and a touch of alcohol. However, what happens when animals catch a scent and indulge in this fermented delight?

Let's begin with nectar. Yeasts, unicellular ascomycete fungi, ubiquitous in insect-pollinated plants, metabolize substantial sugar content within nectar, leading to the production of ethanol and a medley of aromatic compounds. This transformative process mirrors beer brewing, wherein yeasts convert sugars into alcohol, altering the nectar's composition and fragrance.

Scientific studies have highlighted the role of wild yeasts in enhancing floral signaling, influencing the behavior of pollinators. The volatiles and ethanol produced during fermentation act as foraging cues, guiding bees, birds, and other fauna toward nectar sources. A 2023 study by Gareth Thomas and colleagues even found that yeast can supercharge floral communication, making flowers appear brighter and helping pollinators remember their location—benefiting both plant and pollinator!

Picture this: a serene garden abuzz with life. Guided by an exquisite palate, bees pirouette from blossom to blossom, their fuzzy legs adorned with pollen treasures, in search of the sweet embrace of nectar. Unbeknownst to them, every sip of this nectar carries the enchanting essence of wild yeasts, revealing hidden tales through its delicate fragrance. These ethereal cues entice and guide the pollinators, inviting them to partake in nature's subtle brew. Nevertheless, this alluring aroma brings its own set of challenges. While it entices and beckons, the physiological effects of alcohol on these industrious pollinators raise concerns. Imagine bees buzzing a tipsy tune after indulging in the fermented fruits of the floral world. Their motor functioning stops functioning and the poor inebriated bees act goofy, including not getting the waggle dance right when returning to the hive. Engaging in pollination under the influence results in more than just a DUI; it entails punishment from the hive guards, who will sever their legs and abandon the vulnerable bee to its fate.

Hummingbirds too can get tipsy. Consider changing your hummingbird feeder to prevent the nectar or sugar water from fermenting. One study showed that hummingbirds drank half as much when the sugar water contained two percent alcohol. A quick buzz is okay, but not a state of drunkenness. They prefer the designated driver title before flying off.

Butterflies, those flighty beautiful ballerinas of the sky, have no problem getting drunk on fermented nectar. In fact, they appear to seek happy hour. Once drunk, they will remain still in mellow bliss. You can even pick one up since the alcohol deadens their receptors that sense movement. Please, don't add them to your butterfly collection.

Fruit bats, unlike butterflies, don't seek fermented nectar and fruits, but they will enjoy the brew. This is especially true in the summer when fruits are more available and the warmer temperatures speed up the fermentation process. However, even when drinking high amounts of alcohol, the fruit bat can pass the flying-in-a-straight-line sobriety test. Alcohol consumption does not seem to affect their echolocation receptors.

Birds, however, do not seem to hold their liquor. They gorge on fermented blackberries, pyracantha, juniper berries, and crab apples. Take Cedar Waxwings, for example. These beautiful birds love feasting on berries, but sometimes they stumble upon a patch that's gone a little too ripe. A study by Hailu Kinde and colleagues in 2012 documented waxwings actually dying from ethanol poisoning! Blackberries, pyracantha, juniper berries, and crab apples can turn into a boozy trap for unsuspecting birds. These fruits, once fermented, become intoxicating, leading to fatal consequences for birds that overindulge.

Every year we get an onslaught of robins feasting on our pyracantha full of red berries and getting plastered. Despite my efforts to use blue tape as a warning, several birds still hit our window. Leaving water out for sobering them up is an idea and you may even need to keep them in a ventilated box for their own safety. Consider it like holding them captive until they settle bail. Most of the time, they wobble and usually sleep it off. Once the frat party concludes, they depart with no clear hangover.

Dealing with a few drunk birds is one thing, but imagine running across an intoxicated elephant? Elephants are avid consumers of fermented marula fruit, but do they partake in drunken escapades? Not a bar I'd attend. Folklore surrounding elephants' alleged intoxication from marula fruit fermentations has sparked intrigue. Turns out drunken raiding elephants is not true. Researchers like Steve Morris from UC Bristol along with a team at the University of Calgary (2023), looked into this myth. They debunked this notion, attributing the implausibility of intoxication to the sheer size and metabolic capacity of elephants. These gentle giants render the concept of inebriation through fermented fruits an implausible legend. Instead, the elephants partake in the ripe bounty without the fabled intoxicating aftermath.

Many animals have adapted to enjoy the satisfying sugars in fermented fruits without becoming intoxicated. The tree shrew feeds on a regular diet of fermented nectar from bertam palm trees without getting drunk. Its fur contains ethyl glucuronide, a metabolite which absorbs and shows high amounts of alcohol. It has adapted to consume large quantities of alcohol without ill effects.

In his book, *Drunk Flies and Stoned Dolphins*, Oné R. Pagán mentions that several species of those pesky fruit flies, *Drosophila*, have adapted to use alcohol as a defense against parasitic wasps. He notes, "Fruit flies generally display higher resistance to ethanol toxicity than their parasites (more specifically in the case of parasitic wasps, the larval flies display a higher tolerance to ethanol than the wasp larvae)." A game of who can out drink the most. It makes perfect sense that female fruit flies prefer to deposit their eggs in fermented fruits. The higher the concentration of ethanol in the fruit, the more attractive to the egg-laying female.

As we ponder these tipsy tales from the wild, we marvel at the intricate interplay between yeasts, flora, and fauna. It's a saga where fermentation and biodiversity intertwine, where the scent of nectar and fruits becomes an invitation to a nuanced world of flavors, inviting critters to dance along the fine line between intoxication and survival.

A Journey into the Altered States of Consciousness of Animals

Can you imagine an animal that seeks mushrooms to get high? Giorgio Samorini, an ethnobotanist, stands as a pioneer, venturing into the uncharted territory of animal psychedelics. His groundbreaking book, *Animal Psychedelics*, challenges the very foundations of our understanding of consciousness, demonstrating that this profound experience is not exclusive to humans but extends to all living beings. By shedding the limiting cloak of anthropocentrism, he reveals a propensity for altered states of consciousness. Samorini depicts a vibrant scene where creatures pursue and partake in mind-altering substances, from goats on a quest for caffeine to ants engaged in a dance fueled by nectar.

He illuminates the deliberate and conscious engagement of animals with psychedelics. Through his meticulous exploration, Samorini reshapes our perception, challenging the rigid notions that once branded drug use as a negative or pathological behavior. Instead, he offers a paradigm where the consumption of psychedelics becomes a gateway to the evolution of species. He challenges us to view animals, not as mere automatons but as conscious beings, partaking in a quest for altered consciousness that transcends species boundaries.

Let's delve deeper into the captivating realm of animals and mind-altering shrooms. I won't start with the most popular psilocybin and *Amanita muscaria* mushrooms, but in the interesting case of bighorn sheep and lichens. The lichen is a symbiotic relationship between a fungus and an alga or sometimes a cyanobacterium. The fungus protects, hydrates, and anchors the cyanobacterium, while the alga or cyanobacterium provides sugar for the fungus through the process of photosynthesis. But who knew lichen would have hallucinogenic properties? In fact, a rare species of lichen in the Ecuadorian Amazon rainforest provides evidence supporting this possibility. Michaela Schumull, leader of the research involving DNA analysis team identified tryptamine and psilocybin in the lichen, named *Dictyonema huaorani*. In 1981, the discovery of the lichen revealed its composition to be a cyanobacterium and a basidiomycete. Regrettably, the analysis of the sample failed to uncover enough evidence to confirm the presence of hallucinogens. This leaves the question unanswered!

Now back to Bighorn sheep, majestic and resilient beings of the American wilderness. Let's imagine the expansive landscape of the Rockies, where sheer cliffs and perilous paths intertwine. Here, where snow-capped peaks kiss the sky, lies a coveted treasure—a lichen that takes a century to blanket just an inch of rock. A hallucinogenic elixir, thriving in small patches amidst the harsh cliffs and gaps. The captivating green and yellow temptation lures Bighorn sheep. They navigate treacherous ledges and narrow passages, an instinctual pilgrimage in pursuit of their chosen high. They forsake their very teeth, gnashing them against unyielding stone to extract the hallucinogenic lichen. Locals observe the peculiar behavior of these high-seeking mammals. They witness the sheep's solitary voyages, their relentless pursuit of the elusive lichen. The separation from their herds, the risking of life and limb—all in the name of a high that transcends the mundane. Observers note the stark behavioral differences between these lichen-consuming bighorn sheep and their sober counterparts. Given that the lichen provides no nutritional value, it's presumed that the sheep ingest it for its mind-altering effects. Despite anecdotal reports, there is still uncertainty regarding the specifics of this behavior. Records detailing the animals' actions and the identity of the psychoactive lichen are scarce, casting doubt on the veracity of this supposed "Rocky Mountain high."

Whether it's hiking through the Amazon rainforest or mountain climbing to collect samples from the towering Rockies, we must collect enough samples to draw a valid conclusion on the mysteries of psychedelic lichen.

When we think of a mind-altering experience in humans, we think of psilocybin producing mushrooms. While humans often associate these mushrooms with psychedelic trips, scientists are uncovering a surprising twist:

psilocybin may serve as a defense mechanism against pred-ators—specifically, insects. Led by Professor Jason Slot of The Ohio State University, a team of scientists has delved into the intricate relationship between psilocybin and its environment. At its core, psilocybin is a psychoactive compound found in various species of mushrooms across seven genera. The common dung-growing genera includes *Psilocybe* and *Panaeolus*. Nestled within their shared hab-itat, mushrooms and insects engage in a perpetual battle for survival. Insects, lured by the nutrient-rich substrates that foster mushrooms' growth, become both beneficia-ries and threats. The intricacies of insect-mushroom inter-actions reveal a more nuanced tale. The mystery deepens as science delves into the underlying mechanisms of this chemical defense. Psilocybin's role transcends the psyche-delic experiences it inflicts on humans. When these fungi suffer injury, they manifest a telltale blue hue—a response linked to the transformation of psilocybin into psilocin chains.

Within the shared habitat of mushrooms and insects, a perpetual struggle for survival unfolds. The nutrient-rich substrates that support mushroom growth attract insects, who then become both beneficiaries and threats in this delicate ecosystem. When mushrooms are injured, they reveal a telltale blue hue—a sign that psilocybin might be at work. This compound, when transformed into psilocin chains, acts as a potent deterrent to consumption, disrupt-ing the digestive tracts of predators.

But the story doesn't end there. Some insects, like the dark-winged fungus gnat, thrive within psilocybin-rich fruit bodies, utilizing the compound as a safe haven for their own growth. Even leaf-cutter ants incorporate psi-locybin into their nests as a protective shield against adversaries. These examples blur the lines between consumption and utilization, showcasing the complex role psilocybin plays in survival strategies.

Interestingly, while certain mammals, such as deer, have been observed consuming psilocybin mushrooms without apparent harm, the reasons behind this behavior remain a mystery. Do they experience mild psychoactive effects that enhance their foraging abilities or social interactions? The specifics are yet to be understood, leaving us to ponder: if a bear gets "stoned" in the woods, how would we even know?

It's important to note that while some animals might consume psilocybin mushrooms, they may not experience the same psychoactive effects as humans do because of differences in brain chemistry and receptor sensitivity. Animal studies on psilocybin consumption lag far behind the vast research dedicated to its human effects. As research continues to peel back the layers shrouding psilocybin's enigmatic properties, the tale of this compound remains an ever-evolving saga—a story that transcends the boundaries of perception, offering glimpses into the vast expanses of the human mind and those of animals.

Reindeer: Lords of the Tundra, High on Magic Mushrooms

In the freezing vastness of the Arctic tundra, where relentless winds roar and snow covers the land for countless months, the reindeer emerges as a resilient creature. Known as caribou in North America, these members of the deer family are far more than the legendary companions of Santa Claus; they are marvels of adaptation, navigating the harshest environments on Earth with an unparalleled suite of evolutionary tools. Their fur, a marvel of nature's engineering, boasts two layers: a silky undercoat that traps precious warmth and a longer, hollow outer layer acts like a living parka, filled with insulating air. These hairs trap air, creating a barrier against extreme cold.

The reindeer's majestic antlers are striking. They are not only found on males but also on females, which is rare among deer. These tools demonstrate the reindeer's adaptability in sparring and foraging. Even their hooves transform with the seasons, growing broad and concave in winter, perfect for digging through the snowdrifts to unearth hidden feasts of lichen and moss.

Their seasonal migrations, a testament to their adaptability, mark the rhythm of their lives. Traveling hundreds, even thousands, of miles each year, these migrations are a response to the ebb and flow of food availability and weather patterns. In their nomadic journeys, they move as one, aiding in the quest for nourishment. The vast snowy landscapes that might seem desolate to the untrained eye offer a wealth of sustenance for reindeer, from grasses and leaves in the summer to lichens, mosses, and shrub twigs during the harsh winter months. Their remarkable ability to digest these tough, fibrous lichen and plants ensures survival in environments where food is scarce.

Another advantage of traveling in herds is safety in numbers. Predators think twice before tackling a sea of antlers and hooves, and the young, wobbly-legged calves find safety in the watchful eyes of a hundred mothers.

Reindeer, despite their massive size, primarily feed on *Cladonia rangiferina*, nicknamed reindeer moss. *C. rangiferina* is not a moss, but a species of lichen (a fascinating partnership between a fungus and algae!). It forms a thick and crunchy blanket on the ground across the Earth's northern latitudes and helps play an important role in the ecosystem as a food source.

Forget the glowing red nose, reindeer have a secret weapon for navigating the vast, white wilderness: ultraviolet vision. While we struggle to see their favorite snack, *Cladonia rangiferina*, against the snow, these ungulates see it like Dalmatian spots on a purple tablecloth.

Scientists, led by the intrepid Professor Nathaniel Dominy and his team, unraveled this remarkable adaptation. They discovered that reindeer moss, along with their other lichen treats, absorbs ultraviolet (UV) light, while snow acts like a mirror, reflecting it back. This means to a reindeer, the snow glows, making their food stand out in stark contrast.

Reindeer eyes have a special feature called a tapetum, which functions as a built-in headlight, reflecting light back into the eye for better vision in low light. This tapetum also allows UV light to pass through, transforming the winter wonderland into a purple dreamscape for reindeer.

This ability isn't just a seasonal fashion statement. Earlier studies have shown that reindeer's eyes change color throughout the year! In the summer, their tapetum is golden, helping them see in the brighter conditions. But as winter approaches and daylight dwindles, the tapetum shifts to a vivid blue, believed to amplify the low levels of sunlight present during polar winters. This color change, combined with their UV vision, allows reindeer to see their food and navigate their environment even in the harshest conditions.

This UV vision isn't just for finding food. It also helps reindeer spot predators like wolves, whose urine reflects UV light, making them easier to avoid. So, next time you see a reindeer, remember, they're not just munching on lichen; they're having a feast in a world invisible to us mere humans, all thanks to their superpowered, color-changing eyes.

Yet, these resilient beings face their share of challenges. Predators such as wolves, bears, and occasionally wolverines lurk, threatening their existence. Mothers, protective during birthing seasons, guard their vulnerable calves against these perils. Because of climate change, polar bears are switching from their seal diet to a caribou diet. Habitat loss and diseases like chronic wasting disease and brucellosis pose significant threats to various reindeer populations.

These lords of the tundra have a unique appetite. They crave the fly agaric, *Amanita muscaria*. Munching on these potent morsels sends the reindeer on a trip, frolicking in circles, bellowing strange calls, and acting, well, reindeer-ly intoxicated. But why? Some scientists believe the fly agaric holds a secret reindeer pheromone, luring them in with a chemical promise of love and companionship. Others suggest it's an escape, a way to spice up the monotonous lichen diet with a touch of psychedelic pizzazz. Whatever the reason, reindeer have a knack for metabolizing *A. muscaria*'s toxins, leaving behind a potent cocktail of psychoactive compounds. And that's where things get fascinating.

Amanita muscaria has captivated the human imagination for centuries. Its distinctive appearance—a bright red cap adorned with white flecks—makes it instantly recognizable. However, behind its allure lies a complex biology and a cocktail of potent toxins. *Amanita muscaria* is a member of the *Amanita* genus, encompassing a diverse group of mushrooms. It's found in various parts of the Northern Hemisphere, associating itself with coniferous and deciduous trees, forming mycorrhizal relationships wherein the fungus interacts with the tree roots, benefiting both parties.

The mushroom undergoes several stages of development. Initially, it emerges as a small, egg-shaped structure known as the "egg stage," or the volva, eventually expanding into the recognizable mature form with a cap, stem, and gills. The cap color can vary from bright red to orange or even yellow, while the white specks or patches on the cap, remnants of the universal veil, contribute to its distinct appearance. As mentioned earlier, *Amanita muscaria* is the most recognizable mushroom.

Amanita muscaria contains several toxins, the most notable being muscimol and ibotenic acid. These compounds add to its psychoactive effects, albeit quite distinct from those of psilocybin mushrooms. Muscimol is the main psychoactive compound in Amanita muscaria. However, ibotenic acid, which is found in larger amounts, converts to muscimol when ingested. Ibotenic acid itself has neurotoxic properties and can lead to symptoms such as confusion, dizziness, muscle weakness, and, in high doses, seizures and coma. Its conversion to muscimol mitigates some of its toxicity. Muscimol acts as a GABA agonist, binding to GABA receptors and influencing neurotransmission in the central nervous system. This interaction results in sedative, hypnotic, and psychoactive effects. When ingested, muscimol induces alterations in perception, consciousness, and cognitive functions. The combination of these compounds within *Amanita muscaria* results in its unique psychoactive effects. However, the variable and unpredictable nature of these effects, along with the potential for adverse reactions, gastrointestinal distress, and neurological symptoms, underscores the caution needed when dealing with these substances.

Siberian tribes are keen observers of the reindeer's peculiar behavior. They noticed how the animals, after their mushroom-fueled frolics, would urinate a bright yellow liquid. And here's the kicker: that urine, filtered through a reindeer's liver, held an even more potent psychedelic punch than the original mushroom. So began the ancient practice of "drinking the reindeer's wisdom." Urban legend or not? Siberian shamans would feed the fly agaric to their reindeer, then collect the "magic urine" for shamanistic rituals. This potent concoction, free of the mushroom's harsher toxins, propelled them into profound trance states, brimming with visions and spiritual insight.

The reindeer, in their psychedelic revelry, became unwitting guides to the spirit world. Their urine, a bridge between the physical and the metaphysical, facilitated shamanic journeys, seeking knowledge, healing, and connection with the unseen realms. This symbiotic relationship between reindeer and humans, fueled by a mind-altering fungus, speaks volumes about our deep connection with nature. It's a story of adaptation, resourcefulness, and a shared desire to push beyond the boundaries of perception.

Today, the fly agaric's magic continues to captivate us. Scientists are studying its potential for treating addiction and depression. Artists find inspiration in its vibrant form. And the Sami people, descendants of those Siberian shamans, still hold the reindeer sacred, their bond forged in a shared history of altered states and spiritual exploration.

So, the next time you see a reindeer, munching on a red-spotted treat, remember: it might not be just lunch. It might be a portal to another world, a testament to the enduring power of nature's magic and the curious ways we humans find to tap into it.

Epilogue

*The Mayor carries him to the top of Eiffelberg
Tower, where JoJo shouts out a loud 'Yopp!' which
finally makes the kangaroo and the monkeys hear
the Whos. Now convinced of the Whos' existence,
the other jungle animals vow to help Horton
protect the tiny community.*

–Dr. Seuss

We've reached the last note in this captivating exploration of the hidden world where animals and fungi intertwine. I hope this glimpse into fauna funga relationships will make one appreciate their importance to the environment. Better yet, I hope to inspire some of you to continue with your own research in this unexplored field of study.

Remember that childhood spark of fascination with fungi? This journey has taken us far beyond that initial spark, exploring vast ecosystems teeming with creatures big and small, each playing a unique part in nature's grand symphony. We've met the unsung heroes: earthworms enriching the soil, leaf-cutting ants tending their fungal gardens, and countless critters spreading spores like confetti across the landscape.

But the magic goes beyond ecology. It delves into the realm of folklore, medicine, and even altered states of consciousness. From the captivating tales surrounding the fly agaric mushroom to the wisdom of elephants seeking medicinal polypores, we've peeked into the wellspring of ancient knowledge—a testament to the harmony between animals and their natural environment.

However, the melody also carries a somber note. Fauna-Funga partners face a pressing need for protection. The stories of truffle-hunting mammals and mushroom-loving primates serve as poignant reminders of the delicate balance sustaining life on Earth, a balance threatened by habitat loss and human actions. Disturbances are just not at the macro level, but in the unseen world at the micro level. Raking the soil, moving fallen logs or using a leaf blower can cause havoc in communities just as a passing tornado can destroy an entire town. Imagine ourselves in the shoes of Horton from Dr. Seuss' beloved tale, *Horton Hears a Who!* We're not occasional observers: we're the ones who hear the whispers of tiny voices, the intricate whispers of nature's chorus.

Let us shift our perspective. The world is not just a backdrop for animals and fungi; they are integral players in a magnificent performance. Embrace the wonder of nature's diversity. As you venture outdoors, peer beneath fallen leaves, lift a fallen log, listen to the hum of insects, and watch squirrels scampering around mushrooms. Transform your routine walk into a personal safari, revealing connections you may have never noticed before.

With every discovery about the interwoven connections between animal and fungi, we gain a deeper understanding of our role as stewards of this planet. By fostering respect for these relationships and nurturing the natural world, we hold the key to safeguarding the rich mosaic of life for generations to come.

References
and Resources

Prologue/Introduction

Arora, David. 1986. *Mushrooms Demystified*. 2nd ed. Ten Speed Press.

Kendrick, Brice. 2017. *The Fifth Kingdom*. 4th ed. Focus.

Pollan, Michael. 2002. *Botany of Desire*. Random House Trade.

Sagara, Naohiko, Nobuko Tuno, Yu Fukasawa, Shin-ichiro Kawada, and Taiga Kasuya. 2022. "Mushrooms Arising from the Mole Latrine Reveal the Life of Talpid Moles: Proposals of 'Myco-Talpology' and 'Habitat-Cleaning Symbiosis.'" BioRxiv (Cold Spring Harbor Laboratory), October. https://doi.org/10.1101/2022.10.22.513302.

Sheldrake, Merlin. 2021. *Entangled Lives: How Fungi Make Our Worlds, Change Our Minds and Shape Our Futures*. Random House Trade.

Simard, Susan. 2022. *Finding the Mother Tree: Discovering the Wisdom of the Forest*. 1st ed. Vintage.

Vašutová, M., P. Mleczko, A. López-García, I. Maček, G. Boros, J. Ševčík, S. Fujii, D. Hackenberger, I. H. Tuf, E. Hornung, B. Páll-Gergely, and R. Kjøller. 2019. "Taxi Drivers: The Role of Animals in Transporting Mycorrhizal Fungi." *Mycorrhiza* 29 (5): 413–34. https://doi.org/10.1007/s00572-019-00906-1.

Yong, Ed. 2023. *An Immense World: How Animals Sense the Hidden Realms Around Us*. Random House Trade.

Chapter 1: Opening up a Can of Worms; Unveiling the Secret World of Worms and Fungi

Cornell University Mycology Blog. 2006. "Pilobolus and the Lungworm." https://blog.mycology.cornell.edu/2006/12/14/pilobolus-and-the-lungworm/.

Frazer, J. 2021. "How a Carnivorous Mushroom Poisons Its Prey." *Scientific American*, April 8. https://www.scientificamerican.com/article/how-a-carnivorous-mushroom-poisons-its-prey/.

Hadley, Debbie. 2021. "What Are the 5 Types of Insect Larvae?" *ThoughtCo*, February 16. https://www.thoughtco.com/insect-larval-forms-1968484.

Kitchen Garden Magazine. n.d. "Ten Facts About Nematodes." https://www.kitchengarden.co.uk/ten-facts-about-nematodes-e6228pc/.

Lee, Ching-Han, et al. 2020. "Sensory Cilia as the Achilles Heel of Nematodes When Attacked by Carnivorous Mushrooms." *Proceedings of the National Academy of Sciences* 117 (11): 6014–22. https://doi.org/10.1073/pnas.1918473117.

Liebeke, M., N. Strittmatter, S. Fearn, et al. 2015. "Unique Metabolites Protect Earthworms Against Plant Polyphenols." *Nature Communications* 6: 7869. https://doi.org/10.1038/ncomms8869.

Myers, P. 2001. "Nematoda." Animal Diversity Web. Accessed March 22, 2024. https://animaldiversity.org/accounts/Nematoda/.

OpenStax Biology. n.d. "Flatworms, Nematodes, and Arthropods." https://openstax.org/books/concepts-biology/pages/15-3-flatworms-nematodes-and-arthropods.

Pensoft Blog. 2015. "Mysteries in the Mushrooms: First Records of Fungi-Feeding Gnat Larvae from South America." https://blog.pensoft.net/2015/06/11/mysteries-in-the-mushrooms-first-records-of-fungi-feeding-gnat-larvae-from-south-america/.

University of Florida Entomology and Nematology Department. n.d. "Soil Nematodes." https://entnemdept.ufl.edu/creatures/nematode/soil_nematode.htm.

Wikipedia. 2024. "Fictional Depictions of Worms." Last updated January 2024. https://en.wikipedia.org/wiki/Fictional_depictions_of_worms.

Chapter 2: Slow, Slimy, Snails References

Boch, S., D. Prati, S. Werth, J. Rüetschi, and M. Fischer. 2011. "Lichen Endozoochory by Snails." *PLOS ONE* 6 (4): e18770. https://doi.org/10.1371/journal.pone.0018770.

Kitabayashi, K., S. Kitamura, and N. Tuno. 2022. "Fungal Spore Transport by Omnivorous Mycophagous Slug in Temperate Forest." *Ecology and Evolution* 12 (2): e8565. https://doi.org/10.1002/ece3.8565.

Maunder, John E. 2010. "What We Don't Know About Slugs and Mushrooms." *Fungi Magazine* 3.3. https://www.fungimag.com/archives.htm.

Ori, F., M. Menotta, M. Leonardi, A. Amicucci, A. Zambonelli, H. Covès, et al. 2021. "Effect of Slug Mycophagy on Tuber aestivum Spores." *Fungal Biology* 125 (10): 796–805. https://doi.org/10.1016/j.funbio.2021.05.002.

Putra, I., and J. Thamrin. 2021. "Coprinellus sect. Disseminati: Source of Gastropod Mycophagy in Bogor-Indonesia." *Journal of Biota* 6 (3): 147–54. https://doi.org/10.24002/biota.v6i3.3316.

Wedlich, Susanne. 2021. *Slime, A Natural History*. Granta Books.

Chapter 3: A Buzz About Flies and Other Fungi-Loving Arthropods

Cloonan, Kevin R., Stefanos S. Andreadis, Haibin Chen, Nina E. Jenkins, and Thomas C. Baker. 2016. "Attraction, Oviposition and Larval Survival of the Fungus Gnat, Lycoriella ingenua, on Fungal Species Isolated from Adults, Larvae, and Mushroom Compost." *PLoS One* 11 (12): e0167074. https://doi.org/10.1371/journal.pone.0167074.

Cooper Pest Solutions. 2007. "What Are the Tiny Jumping Bugs in My House?" https://ipm.ucanr.edu/PMG/PESTNOTES/pn74136.html.

Cornell Mycology Blog. 2011. "Postal Conks and the Forked Fungus Beetle." https://blog.mycology.cornell.edu/2011/09/16/postal-conks/.

Kecskemeti, Sandor, et al. 2020. "Fungal Volatiles as Olfactory Cues for Female Fungus Gnat, Lycoriella ingenua in the Avoidance of Mycelia Colonized Compost." *Journal of Chemical Ecology* 46 (10): 917–26. https://doi.org/10.1007/s10886-020-01210-5.

Chapter 4: Social Insects: Industrial Mushroom Farmers

Aanen, D. K., V. I. Ros, H. H. de Fine Licht, J. Mitchell, Z. W. de Beer, B. Slippers, C. Rouland-Lefèvre, and J. J. Boomsma. 2007. "Patterns of Interaction Specificity of Fungus-Growing Termites and Termitomyces Symbionts in South Africa." *BMC Evolutionary Biology* 7: 115. https://doi.org/10.1186/1471-2148-7-115.

Bunyard, Britt A. 2022. *The Lives of Fungi: A Natural History of Our Planet's Decomposers*. 1st ed. Princeton University Press.

Kendrick, Brice. 2017. *The Fifth Kingdom*. 4th ed. Focus.

Montoya, Q. V., M. J. S. Martiarena, D. A. Polezel, S. Kakazu, and A. Rodrigues. 2019. "More Pieces to a Huge Puzzle: Two New *Escovopsis* Species from Fungus Gardens of Attine Ants." *MycoKeys* 46: 1–22. https://doi.org/10.3897/mycokeys.46.30951.

Salvo, Michael. n.d. "Leaf Cutter Ants." Elegant Entomology. https://elegantentomology.weebly.com/leaf-cutter-ants.html.

University of Freiburg. 2022. "Ambrosia Beetles Breed and Maintain Their Own Food Fungi." *Phys.org*. https://phys.org/news/2022-11-ambrosia-beetles-food-fungi.html.

Wikipedia. 2022. "Aradidae." https://en.wikipedia.org/wiki/Aradidae.

Wikipedia. 2022. "Ambrosia Beetle." https://en.wikipedia.org/wiki/Ambrosia_beetle.

Chapter 5: The Poop Squad (Coprophilous Fungi)

Blackman, Stuart. 2022. "Discover the Fascinating Fungus *Pilobolus crystallinus* Aka 'Dung Cannon.'" *Discover Wildlife Magazine*. https://www.discoverwildlife.com/plant-facts/fungi/pilobolus-crystallinus-dung-cannon.

Boddy, Lynne, Nicholas Money, and Sarah C. Watkinson. 2016. *The Fungi*. 3rd ed. Academic Press.

Kuo, M. 2007. "Panaeolus papilionaceus." *MushroomExpert.Com*. http://www.mushroomexpert.com/panaeolus_papilionaceus.html.

Leech, Tony. 2023. "The Dung-Lovers: An Introduction to Coprophilous Fungi." YouTube. British Mycological Society. https://www.youtube.com/watch?v=9zAa-ifXRSE.

Mungai, P. G., J. G. Njogu, E. Chukeatirote, and K. D. Hyde. 2012. "Coprophilous Ascomycetes in Kenya: *Sporormiella* from Wildlife Dung." *Mycology* 3 (4): 234–51. https://doi.org/10.1080/21501203.2012.752413.

Richardson, M. J. 2018. *Keys to Fungi on Dung*. British Mycological Society. Project Gutenberg Ebook. https://flexpub.com/epubs/pg57291-images/OEBPS/@public@vhost@g@gutenberg@html@files@57291@57291-h@57291-h-0.htm.html.

Wikipedia. n.d. "Coprophilous Fungi." https://en.wikipedia.org/wiki/Coprophilous_fungi.

Chapter 6: Pollinators and Fungi: Unveiling Their Interwoven Relationship

BeeAware. n.d. "Varroa Mites." https://beeaware.org.au/archive-pest/varroa-mites.

Chaverri, P., and G. Chaverri. 2022. "Fungal Communities in Feces of the Frugivorous Bat *Ectophylla alba* and Its Highly Specialized *Ficus colubrinae* Diet." *Animal Microbiome* 4: 24. https://doi.org/10.1186/s42523-022-00169-w.

DeMarco, Emily. 2015. "Fungi Can Help Monarchs Self-Medicate by Changing Milkweed Chemistry, Soil Microbes Alter the Spread of a Crippling Monarch Parasite." *Science*. https://www.science.org/content/article/fungi-can-help-monarchs-self-medicate.

Entomology Today. 2015. "Root Fungi on Milkweed Affects Monarch Butterfly Health." https://entomologytoday.org/2015/10/14/root-fungi-on-milkweed-plants-affect-monarch-butterfly-health/.

Han, J. O., N. L. Naeger, B. K. Hopkins, et al. 2021. "Directed Evolution of *Metarhizium* Fungus Improves Its Biocontrol Efficacy Against *Varroa* Mites in Honey Bee Colonies." *Scientific Reports* 11: 10582. https://doi.org/10.1038/s41598-021-89811-2.

Lara, C., and J. F. Ornelas. 2023. "Hummingbirds as Vectors of Fungal Spores in *Moussonia deppeana* (Gesneriaceae): Taking Advantage of a Mutualism?" *American Journal of Botany*. https://doi.org/10.3732/ajb.90.2.262.

Nishida, Kenji, and Robert K. Robbins. 2020. "One Side Makes You Taller: A Mushroom–Eating Butterfly Caterpillar (Lycaenidae) in Costa Rica." *Neotropical Biology and Conservation* 15 (4): 463–70. https://doi.org/10.3897/neotropical.15.e57998.

Schattenberg, Paul. 2022. "Monarch Butterflies Facing Battle For Survival, Experts Say." Texas A&M AgriLife Communications. https://today.tamu.edu/2022/08/02/monarch-butterflies-facing-battle-for-survival-experts-say/.

Stamets, P. E., N. L. Naeger, J. D. Evans, et al. 2018. "Extracts of Polypore Mushroom Mycelia Reduce Viruses in Honey Bees." *Scientific Reports* 8: 13936. https://doi.org/10.1038/s41598-018-32194-8.

Tao, L., C. D. Gowler, A. Ahmad, M. D. Hunter, and J. C. de Roode. 2015. "Disease Ecology Across Soil Boundaries: Effects of Below-Ground Fungi on Above-Ground Host-Parasite Interactions." *Proceedings of the Royal Society B: Biological Sciences* 282 (1817): 20151993. https://doi.org/10.1098/rspb.2015.1993.

Washington State University. 2021. "Fungus Fights Mites That Harm Honey Bees." *ScienceDaily.* https://www.sciencedaily.com/releases/2021/05/210527091441.htm.

Chapter 7: Connecting the Dots: Exploring the Link Between Herpetology and Mycology

Cooper, T., and K. Vermes. 2011. "Mycophagy in the Larger Bodied Skinks of the Genera *Tiliqua* and *Egernia*: Are Their Implications for Ecosystem Health?" *Australian Zoologist* 35: 681–84.

Elliott, Todd F. 2019. "Reptilian Mycophagy: A Global Review of Mutually Beneficial Associations Between Reptiles and Macrofungi." *Mycosphere.*

Jones, S. C., W. J. Jordan IV, S. J. Meiners, A. N. Miller, and A. S. Methven. 2007. "Fungal Spore Dispersal by the Eastern Box Turtle (Terrapene carolina carolina)." *The American Midland Naturalist* 157 (1): 121–26.

Kane, Aurora. 2023. *Mystical Mushrooms, Discover the Magic and Folklore of Fantastic Fungi.* Quartro Publishing Group.

Millman, Lawrence. 2019. *Fungipedia, A Brief Compendium of Mushroom Lore.* Princeton University Press.

Morell, Virginia. 2016. "Fungus Turns Frogs into Sexy Zombies." *Science.* https://www.science.org/content/article/fungus-turns-frogs-sexy-zombies.

Chapter 8: A Glimpse into the World of Bird-Fungi Relationships

Berger, Cynthia. 2012. "True Colors: How Birds See the World, Thanks to UV Vision, Birds See the World Very Differently Than We Do." *National Wildlife Federation.* https://www.nwf.org/Magazines/National-Wildlife/2012/AugSept/Animals/Bird-Vision.

Borgia, G. 1995. "Why Do Bowerbirds Build Bowers?" *American Scientist* 83 (6): 542–47. [invalid URL removed].

Caiafa, M. V., M. A. Jusino, A. C. Wilkie, I. A. Díaz, K. E. Sieving, and M. E. Smith. 2021. "Discovering the Role of Patagonian Birds in the Dispersal of Truffles and Other Mycorrhizal Fungi." *Current Biology* 31 (24): 5558–70.e3. https://doi.org/10.1016/j.cub.2021.10.024.

Elliott, T. F., M. A. Jusino, J. M. Trappe, H. Lepp, G. Ballard, J. J. Bruhl, and K. Vernes. 2019. "A Global Review of the Ecological Significance of Symbiotic Associations Between Birds and Fungi." *Fungal Diversity* 98: 161–94. [https://www.fs.usda.gov/nrs/pubs/jrnl/2021/nrs_2021_caiafa_001.pdf.

Elliott, T. F., and P. A. Marshall. 2016. "Animal-Fungal Interactions 1: Notes on Bowerbird's Use of Fungi." *Australian Zoologist*. https://doi.org/10.7882/AZ.2015.032.

Morell, Virginia. 2016. "Woodpeckers Partner with Fungi to Build Homes. Wood-Eating Fungus Helps Birds Dig Holes in Trees." *Science*. https://www.science.org/content/article/woodpeckers-partner-fungi-build-homes.

Norris, Ann. 2022. "10 Bioluminescent Mushrooms That Glow in the Dark." *Treehugger*. https://www.treehugger.com/bioluminescent-fungi-mushrooms-that-glow-in-the-dark-4868794.

Runwal, Priyanka. 2020. "Truffles Aren't Just for Foodies—Some Birds Love Them, Too." *Audubon Magazine*. https://www.audubon.org/news/truffles-arent-just-foodies-some-birds-love-them-too.

Wikipedia contributors. 2024. "List of Bioluminescent Fungi." *Wikipedia, The Free Encyclopedia*. https://en.wikipedia.org/w/index.php?title=List_of_bioluminescent_fungi&oldid=1219354622.

Chapter 9: Mammalian Mycophagy
(Furry Fungal Feeders)

Animal Diversity Web. n.d. "Myodes gapperi." Accessed 2023. https://animaldiversity.org/accounts/Myodes_gapperi/.

Caiafa, P., M. A. M. Aguiar, and J. B. Sanseverino. 2000. "Dispersal of Hypogeous Fungi by Mammals: A Review." *Brazilian Journal of Biology* 60 (3): 493–504.

Claridge, A., and R. M. May. 1994. "The Role of Mammals in

the Dispersal of Truffles." *Australian Journal of Ecology* 19 (1): 1–11.

Claridge, A. W., and J. M. Trappe. 2005. "Sporocarp Mycophagy: Nutritional, Behavioral, Evolutionary, and Physiological Aspects." In *The Fungal Community*, 3rd ed., edited by J. Dighton, J. F. White, and P. Oudemans, 503–7. Boca Raton, FL: CRC Press.

Elliott, J. E., E. W. Schupp, and A. Claridge. 2019. "The Role of Mammals in Fungal Spore Dispersal: A Global Review of Ecosystem Interactions." *Fungal Ecology* 37: 77–92.

Elliott, T. F., C. Truong, S. Jackson, C. L. Zúñiga, J. M. Trappe, and K. Vernes. 2022a. "Mammalian Mycophagy: A Global Review of Ecosystem Interactions Between Mammals and Fungi." *Fungal Systematics and Evolution* 9: 99–159. https://doi.org/10.3114/fuse.2022.09.07.

Elliott, T. F., C. Truong, S. Jackson, C. L. Zúñiga, J. M. Trappe, and K. Vernes. 2022b. "Mammalian Mycophagy: Global Review of Ecosystem Interactions Between Mammals and Fungi." *Fungal.* https://www.ncbi.nlm.nih.gov/pmc/articles/PMC9402283/.

Feder, Sylvia. 2011. "Nature on Trail: Flying Squirrels, Fungi and Forests." *Washington Trails Magazine.* https://www.wta.org/hiking-info/nature-on-trail/nature-on-trail-flying-squirrels-fungi-and-forests.

Horton, Chris. 2023. "This Is How Dogs Learn to Hunt for Truffles." *National Geographic.* https://www.nationalgeographic.com/travel/article/how-dogs-learn-to-hunt-for-truffles.

Johnson, C. N. 1996. "Interactions Between Mammals and Ectomycorrhizal Fungi." *Trends in Ecology and Evolution* 11: 503–7.

Luoma, D. L., J. M. Trappe, A. W. Claridge, K. M. Jacobs, and E. Cazares. 2003. "Relationships Among Fungi and Small Mammals in Forested Ecosystems." In *Forest Mammals: Biology and Management*, edited by C. J. Zabel and R. G. Anthony, 273-286. Humbolt State University.

Meyer, M., M. North, and D. Kelt. 2005. "Fungi in the Diets of Northern Flying Squirrels and Lodgepole Chipmunks in the Sierra Nevada." *Canadian Journal of Zoology.* https://www.sierraforestlegacy.org/Resources/Conservation/SierraNevadaWildlife/NorthernFlyingSquirrel/NFS-Meyer05b.pdf.

Orrock, J. L., and J. F. Pagels. 2002. "Fungus Consumption by the Southern Red-Backed Vole (Clethrionomys Gapperi) in the Southern Appalachians." *The American Midland Naturalist* 147 (2): 413–18. [invalid URL removed].

Piattoni, Federica, Francesca Ori, Antonella Amicucci, Elena Salerni, and Alessandra Zambonelli. 2016. "Interrelationships Between Wild Boars (Sus scrofa) and Truffles." https://doi.org/10.1007/978-3-319-31436-5_22.

Ryan B. Stephens, Benjamin Borgmann-Winter, Rebecca J. Rowe. 2023. "Linking Small Mammals, Mycorrhizal Fungi, and Forest Regeneration." https://www.takingactionfor-wildlife.org/blog/2023/05/linking-small-mammals-mycor-rhizal-fungi-forest-regeneration.

Schickmann, S., A. Urban, K. Kräutler, et al. 2012. "The Interrelationship of Mycophagous Small Mammals and Ectomycorrhizal Fungi in Primeval, Disturbed and Managed Central European Mountainous Forests." *Oecologia* 170: 395–409. https://doi.org/10.1007/s00442-012-2303-2.

Schiestl, F. P. 2004. "Fungal Spore Dispersal by Animals: A Review." *Fungal Biology Reviews* 18 (1-2): 1–20.

Schupp, E. W., J. E. Elliott, and A. Claridge. 2010. "Mammalian Mycophagy and Ecosystem Functioning." In *Fungal Ecology*, 395–415. Elsevier.

Stephens, R. B., and R. J. Rowe. 2020. "Neglected Role of Rodent Generalists in Fungal Spore Dispersal Networks." *Ecology*. https://doi.org/10.1002/ecy.2972.

Tapir Specialist Group. 2017. "All about the Terrific Tapir Specialist Group." Tapir Specialist Group. 2017. https://tapirs.org/tapirs/.

Trappe, J. M., and A. W. Claridge. 2005. "Hypogeous Fungi: Evolution of Reproductive and Dispersal Strategies Through Interactions with Animals and Mycorrhizal Plants." In *The Fungal Community*, 3rd ed., edited by J. Dighton, J. F. White, and P. Oudemans, 395–409. Boca Raton, FL: CRC Press.

Vernes, K., and L. Dunn. 2009. "Mammal Mycophagy and Fungal Spore Dispersal Across a Steep Environmental Gradient in Eastern Australia." *Austral Ecology* 34 (1): 69–76.

Waters, Jeffrey, Kevin McKelvey, Cynthia Zabel, and Daniel Luoma. 2000. "Northern Flying Squirrel Mycophagy and Truffle Production in Fir Forests in Northeastern California." USDA Forest Service.

Chapter 10: Mushroom Munching Monkeys

Abrams, Sylvie. 2018. "Yunnan Snub-Nosed Monkey *Rhino-pithecus bieti*." Ne Primate Conservancy. https://neprimate-conservancy.org/yunnan-snub-nosed-monkey/.

Elliott, T. F., A. V. Georgiev, A. L. Lokasola, and M. E. Smith. 2020. "*Hysterangium bonobo*: A Newly Described Truffle Species That Is Eaten by Bonobos in the Democratic Republic of Congo." *Mycologia* 112 (6): 1203–11. https://doi.org/10.1080/0 0275514.2020.1790234.

Grueter, C. C., D. Li, B. Ren, F. Wei, and C. P. van Schaik. 2009. "Dietary Profile of *Rhinopithecus bieti* and Its Socioecological Implications." *International Journal of Primatology* 30 (4): 601–24. https://doi.org/10.1007/s10764-009-9363-0.

Hanson, A. M., K. T. Hodge, and L. M. Porter. 2003. "Mycology Among Primates."

Mycologist. https://doi.org/10.1017/S0269915X0300106X.

Li, Yunqi. 2019. "Monkey Mania: The Yunnan Snub-Nosed Monkey." CGTN. https://news.cgtn.com/news/189510-2/index.html.

Mountain Marmosets Conservation Program. 2022. "The Battle to Save the Buffy Tufted Marmoset of Brazil." Earth.Org. https://earth.org/buffy-tufted-marmoset-of-brazil/.

The Guardian. 2017. https://www.theguardian.com/science/2017/mar/08/neanderthal-dental-tartar-reveals-plant-based-diet-and-drugs.

Xiang, Z. F., S. Huo, W. Xiao, R. C. Quan, and C. C. Grueter. 2007. "Diet and Feeding Behavior of *Rhinopithecus bieti* at Xiaochangdu, Tibet: Adaptations to a Marginal Environment." *American Journal of Primatology* 69 (10): 1141–58. https://doi.org/10.1002/ajp.20412.

Yang, Y., A. K. Lin, P. A. Garber, Z. Huang, Y. Tian, A. Behie, F. Momberg, C. C. Grueter, W. Li, N. Lwin, and W. Xiao. 2022. "The 10th Anniversary of the Scientific Description of the Black Snub-Nosed Monkey (*Rhinopithecus strykeri*): It Is Time to Initiate a Set of New Management Strategies to Save This Critically Endangered Primate from Extinction." *American Journal of Primatology*. https://doi.org/10.1002/ajp.23372.

**Chapter 11: Nature Apothecaries: Animals
That Seek Medicinal Mushrooms**

Higginbotham, S., W. R. Wong, R. G. Linington, C. Spadafora, L. Iturrado, et al. 2014. "Sloth Hair as a Novel Source of Fungi with Potent Anti-Parasitic, Anti-Cancer and Anti-Bacterial Bioactivity." *PLoS ONE.* [1] https://doi.org/10.1371/journal.pone.0084549.

Patterson, Garreth. 2010. *The Secret Elephants: The Rediscovery of the World's Most Southerly Elephants.* Penguin Global.

Rojas-Gätjens, Diego, Katherine S. Valverde-Madrigal, Keilor Rojas-Jimenez, Reinaldo Pereira, Judy Avey-Arroyo, and Max Chavarría. 2022. "Antibiotic-producing Micrococcales Govern the Microbiome That Inhabits the Fur of Two- and Three-toed Sloths." https://doi.org/10.1111/1462-2920.16082.

Rojas-Gätjens, D., J. Avey-Arroyo, P. Chaverri, K. Rojas-Jimenez, and M. Chavarría. 2023. "Differences in Fungal Communities in the Fur of Two- and Three-toed Sloths." *Microbiology.* https://doi.org/10.1099/mic.0.001309.

Chapter 12: Drunk and or Stoned on Fungi

Alex, Bridget. 2020. "Drunken Monkey' Hypothesis: Was Booze an Advantage For Our Ancestors?" *Discover.* https://www.discovermagazine.com/planet-earth/drunken-monkey-hypothesis-was-booze-an-advantage-for-our-ancestors.

Altamirano, Marco. 2023. "Do Animals Get Drunk?" *Nautilus.* https://nautil.us/do-animals-get-drunk-306357/.

Animal Cognition. 2015. "Animal Drug Use." http://www.animalcognition.org/2015/05/16/animal-drug-use/.

Awan, Ali R., Jaclyn M. Winter, Daniel Turner, William M. Shaw, Laura M. Suz, Alexander J. Bradshaw, Tom Ellis, and Bryn T.M. Dentinger. 2018. "Convergent Evolution of Psilocybin Biosynthesis by Psychedelic Mushrooms." https://doi.org/10.1101/374199.

Big Think. 2018. "Do Moose and Other Animals Eat Fermented Fruit to Get Drunk?" https://bigthink.com/big-think-books/do-moose-and-other-animals-eat-fermented-fruit-to-get-drunk/.

Evans, Robert. 2009. "7 Species That Get High More Than We Do." http://www.cracked.com/article_17032_7-species-that-get-high-more-than-we-do.html#ixzz3Kw2Ft5ru.

Gabbatiss, Josh. 2018. "Magic Mushrooms Evolved Hallucinogenic Chemicals to Stop Insects Eating Them, Say Scientists." *Independent*. https://www.independent.co.uk/news/science/magic-mushrooms-hallucinogenic-chemical-properties-insects-eat-defensive-measure.

Graber, Cynthia. 2008. "Fact or Fiction: Animals Like to Get Drunk." *Scientific American*. https://www.scientificamerican.com/article/animals-like-to-get-drunk/.

Huffman, Michael A. 2003. "Animal Self-Medication and Ethnobotany: Exploring the Origins of Human Pharmacopoeias." https://pubmed.ncbi.nlm.nih.gov/14506884/.

Janish, S. 2024. "M. reukaufii: A Nectar-Inhabiting Wild Yeast with Biotransformation Potential in Hoppy Beer." Scott Janish. https://scottjanish.com/m-reukaufii-a-nectar-inhabiting-wild-yeast-with-biotransformation-potential-in-hoppy-beer/.

Natura Mushrooms. 2020. "Amanita Muscaria: The Fascinating History Of The Fairy Tale Fungus." https://naturamushrooms.com/blogs/news/amanita-muscaria-the-fascinating-history-of-the-fairy-tale-fungus.

Opar, Alissa. 2011. "Spring Air and So Are Intoxicated Birds." National Audubon Society. https://www.audubon.org/news/spring-air-and-so-are-intoxicated-birds.

Pagan, One R. 2021. *Drunk Flies and Stoned Dolphins: A Trip Through the World of Animal Intoxication*. BenBella Books.

Reynolds, Hannah T., Vinod Vijayakumar, Emile Gluck-Thaler, Hailee Brynn Korotkin, Patrick Brandon Matheny, and Jason C. Slot. 2018. "Horizontal Gene Cluster Transfer Increased Hallucinogenic Mushroom Diversity." https://doi.org/10.1002/evl3.42.

Samorini, Giorgio. 2002. *Animals and Psychedelics: The Natural World and the Instinct to Alter Consciousness*. Park Street Press.

Save the Bees. 2023. "Yes Bees Can Get Drunk." https://savannahbee.com/blogs/the-latest-buzz/yes-bees-can-get-drunk.

Schmull, Michaela, Manuela Dal-Forno, Robert Lücking, Shugeng Cao, Jon Clardy, and James D. Lawrey. 2014. "*Dictyonema huaorani* (Agaricales: Hygrophoraceae),[1] a New Lichenized Basidiomycete from Amazonian Ecuador with Presumed Hallucinogenic Properties." *The Bryologist*. http://doi.org/10.1639/0007-2745-117.4.386.

Solis-Moreira, J. 2023. "Too Drunk to Fly? Hummingbirds Are Guzzling Alcohol in Flowers and Bird Feeders." *StudyFinds*. https://studyfinds.org/hummingbirds-alcohol/.

University of Calgary. 2020. "Elephants Get Drunk Because They Can't Metabolize Alcohol." https://ucalgary.ca/news/elephants-get-drunk-because-they-cant-metabolize-alcohol-us.

Umhauer, Natasha. 2015. "9 Animals That Could Teach Us Something About Drugs and Alcohol." *BuzzFeed*. https://www.buzzfeed.com/natashaumer/9-animals-that-could-teach-us-something-about-drugs-and-alco.

Will, Melissa J. 2020. "Do Animals Get Drunk?" *Empress of Dirt*. https://empressofdirt.net/do-animals-get-drunk/.

Acknowledgements

Many thanks to all who contributed to the publication of my book *Animal Mycophiles: Critters that Hunt, Farm, Self-medicate, and Get High from Fungi.* The unseen bonds of a forest's mycelial network mirror the support you gave me, enabling me to create a book that helps readers understand these critical relationships.

To Dede Cummings at Green Writer's Press, my deepest gratitude for nurturing this project from spore to mushroom. Your sketches were like detailed field notes, capturing the essence of these partnerships. Beyond our professional collaboration, your friendship has been a treasure discovered along the way.

Maria Tane, my developmental editor, your keen eye, and thoughtful suggestions, allowed the core ideas to flourish. Our partnership transformed the initial primordia of this manuscript into the rich fruiting body I now hold. Thank you for embracing the subtle humor, in introducing these wonders to a wider audience. And to Marissa Graf, your meticulous copy-editing was the crucial final touch, ensuring each detail shone with clarity.

Cover designer Allison Pineault, the artistry you crafted, captures the often-unseen yet profound partnerships between animals and fungi. The cover is a visual echo of the book's central theme.

To my dear friends and partners in mycology education, Melany Kahn, and Jennifer Hall, you were vital nutrients in this creative ecosystem. Melany, your introduction to Green Writer's Press was the pivotal moment that set my book's publication in motion. And your own inspiring book, *Mason Goes Mushrooming,* is spreading the spores of mycological curiosity in young minds. Jennifer, your beta reading provided essential early insights, like the first hyphae reaching for support. Our shared worldview deepens our friendship, a bond as strong and enduring as an ancient mycelial network.

I'm deeply grateful to the mycology community for sharing their vast knowledge and opening my eyes to the wonders of fungi. Your books inspired my awe with every detailed description and breathtaking photograph.

To my husband, Drew, and family, your unwavering support was the stable substrate upon which this project could grow. Special gratitude to my beloved Rose and Michael, the next generation of earth stewards.

To the boundless inspiration of nature, for the quiet moments that allowed me to observe and appreciate the intricate web of life that surrounds us.

ABOUT THE AUTHOR

EVA GORDON, a former science teacher with twenty years' experience, now shares her passion for the natural world through her nonfiction work on animal mycophiles. On the Education Committee for the North American Mycological Association, she is dedicated to spreading the word (spores) about mycology. Eva is a sought-after speaker, captivating audiences of all ages with her insights into the fascinating world of animal mycophiles and mycology for educators. Eva lives in the Pacific Northwest with her husband and their Wire-haired Fox Terrier. She enjoys hiking, forest bathing, and reveling in the magic of the natural world.